glossolalia, p. 37f

Aesklepius, 70 + 71, 94

"fate" for "faith" — 79

"throw" — p. 81

"boy" – for servant. – p. 95

"decensus" for "descensus" p. 116, 152, 223

"advantaged", p. 119

Isocrates ad Nicolem, p. 160 – Nicoclem

EARLY CHRISTIAN LIFE

EARLY CHRISTIAN LIFE

AS REFLECTED IN ITS LITERATURE

By DONALD WAYNE RIDDLE

The University of Chicago

WILLETT, CLARK & COMPANY

CHICAGO   NEW YORK

1936

To

ROBERT EMERY RIDDLE

MY SON

PREFACE

This volume makes an approach to the historical study of early Christianity which is new in that it relegates doctrine and teaching as quite secondary, while it utilizes literature as source for the study of early Christian life, rather than as an end in itself. It does, indeed, make use of the framework and sequence of early Christian literature. This is in response to the judgment that it is necessary to illustrate in practice what is deemed to be the proper method of using literary sources: i.e., the social approach. It will be observed as an essential principle that no difference is made between New Testament and extra-New Testament sources; early Christian literature arose from early Christian life, and there is no distinction in kind between the sources which are in the New Testament and those which do not have that status. This study is based upon the conviction that the essential feature in the growth of Christianity is the Christian life. Detailed points in the study of the New Testament and of the history of the early church must be built upon this foundation.

In the author's view the most important contribution of the present study is to be found in the picture of the types of the religious life which are reconstructed from the study of the gospels and the several pictures, so fascinating in their contrasts, developed from the materials of the later books of the New Testament and from contemporaneous sources. It is a distinct need in modern study that the gospels be interrogated vitally rather than mechanically; it is now essential that their information of the life which produced them be made available. Theories of source and of form cannot be allowed to stop short of the discovery of the processes of the growth of the gospel materials and of the extremely human adventures and experiments in living which they reflect. Likewise the secrets of the later sources must be yielded by their study from the viewpoint of early Christian life. This book is an attempt to explore what has been discovered to be a rich field. It is hoped that it is successful at least in suggesting the interest of the materials and the value of the approach.

The author wishes to express his thanks to Mr. Harold H. Hutson for assistance in proofreading. To his friend, Dr. Martin Rist, he is also indebted for reading the typescript and for making valuable suggestions.

DONALD WAYNE RIDDLE

THE UNIVERSITY OF CHICAGO
July 14, 1936

CONTENTS

PART ONE

BEFORE THE GOSPELS

BEGINNINGS

Christianity began when certain followers of Jesus, and others after them, had experiences which led them to believe that the crucified Jesus was alive again. They were impelled to talk about these experiences. In response to their stories, little groups of people came to be associated together on the basis of this common interest. Since they were characterized by remarkable enthusiasm, fellowships based upon these beliefs and interests had quick growth.

The followers of Jesus were Jewish, as he was. It was natural, then, that those who had these remarkable experiences, and those who first heard their stories, were Jewish. As judged by usual Jewish standards of their time and place they seem to have been " peculiar " persons, for it was not common for Jews of ancient Palestine to have such experiences. Possibly they were unusual in other respects, also.[1]

However, they seem to have been willing to tell their stories to anyone who would listen. Thus others than Jews heard them, and others than Jews believed them. This is shown by the fact that when these matters came to the attention of unsympathetic religious leaders the fellowships had spread geographically, grown numerically, and become inclusive of other racial groups.

This is a simple fact. But its consequence was of profound importance. There were many peoples and many religions in the world into which Christianity came. It is of the greatest significance that early Christianity began within Judaism but quickly became inclusive of non-Jews; that early in its growth there were fellowships in the Jewish villages and cities of Palestine and in the Hellenistic cities of Palestine and of the wider Graeco-Roman world. The meaning of the early currency of Christianity in Hellenistic centers is apparent to anyone who regards the influence of environment as important.

The next fact to be pointed out is even more arresting. Since the early Christian leaders were accustomed to tell their stories about Jesus to any who would listen, and since from an early time those who heard and believed included Jews and non-Jews, and since the stories were told in Jewish and Hellenistic circles within and outside Palestine, a variety of response occurred. It has been noted that Jewish people who " saw " the risen Jesus may have been untypical Jews. While most Jews at this time believed in life after death, and while many believed that sometime God would raise people from the dead, it was extraordinary for a Jew to believe that God had recently raised one certain person from the dead. Of course, it was easy for later Christians to explain how God raised Jesus and caused him to appear to Peter and others. Nevertheless it was unusual for a Jew of ancient Palestine to have had the experiences attributed to Peter and others, and difficult for Jews to believe the stories which were told.

On the other hand, non-Jews of the Hellenistic world were very familiar with tales of risen heroes. The religious lore of the Hellenistic peoples had made them current. It was but natural, then, that a readier response to the stories about Jesus was made by non-Jews. Likewise, Hellenistic Jews were presumably more likely to listen and accept them than were Jews of Palestine.

Further, some [2] members of the fellowships formed by the believers were characterized by particular aspects of behavior. They acted upon the conviction that they had immediate access to God, and that God inspired them and thus impelled them to do marvelous things. Thus they came to be regarded as " peculiar "; it was not long until their ways of living, as well as their oft-repeated stories of Jesus, marked them as different, and presently made them unpopular with many of their neighbors.

On the other hand, these characteristics met with less hostile reactions from others. Here, again, there was a difference between Palestinian Jews and Hellenists. Many of the gentiles were used to such behavior, and regarded it as usual in the religious life. Examples of the spiritistic behavior then and later alleged of Christians were well known in the Hellenistic religions. Doubtless this largely explains why non-Jews early came into the fellowships, and why it was not long until there were more non-Jews than Jews in them. Again, this makes it understandable that fellowships were early found beyond Galilee and Jerusalem and outside Palestine.

It was inevitable that soon the question would be raised whether the non-Jews in the fellowships must conform to Jewish practices. It was important for the future of Christianity that this question was not raised until the number and the proportion of non-Jews were considerable, and until there were a number of fellowships in extra-Palestinian territories.

For when the question was raised the fellowships were

already racially inclusive. They had no racial or national character. In so far as the religious life of the adherents was characteristic it was thoroughly individual. The benefits conferred by believing the stories about Jesus, or by belonging to the fellowship, were all with reference to the individual. This was basically different from Judaism; it was fundamental in Judaism that the whole people was the religious unit: Israel was the Lord's people, and he was Lord of Israel. The benefits of the Jewish religious life were likewise with reference to the group. It was impossible to belong to the Jewish religion without belonging to the Jewish people — this is the essential significance of circumcision. But since the fellowships of the stories of Jesus were racially inclusive, without racial or national basis — the stories told to all who would hear, the benefits available to everyone who responded — it was but natural that in the spread of the fellowships their inclusion of more non-Jews than Jews and their presence in Hellenistic communities largely determined their character.

The next step in Christianity's growth was the aggressive offer of its messages and its benefits to non-Jews in their own localities. Probably the beginnings of this new departure were, so to speak, accidental, or at least adventitious.[3] Travelers or other migrants took their stories with them; doubtless many of these were so enthusiastic that they spread the good news wherever they went. The missionary character of early Christianity was inherent from the very earliest times.

Local cults were, presumably, based upon the stories of Jesus which had grown out of the primary experiences of those who had "witnessed" Jesus' "resurrection." Not every messenger had had the experience; the list of "appearances " given by Paul (1 Cor. 15:5-8) is an interesting and an important datum, but these few dramatic experiences were not the sole foundation of the quickly spreading fellow-ships. Many a humble and obscure believer, although no " appearance " had been vouchsafed him, had in his enthusiasm and in the power of the story which he had heard from another and repeated in his own words enough to make him an effective agent in spreading the good news. Both the conspicuous leader and the humble follower were important in Christianity's growth; there is something infectious in the religious experience of any person when it is vital and when it is told with enthusiasm.

At all events, within a few years after the death of Jesus there were societies of his followers not only in Palestine but in many localities of the eastern and the northeastern Mediterranean shore. Several leaders had identified themselves with the movement which was now well under way. Widespread geographically, the cults were likewise inclusive of people who had diverse racial or national origin and were thoroughly individualistic in their religious lives. What was to become Christianity was a lively, going movement, a sign of whose life was a ready adaptability to the needs which particular problems or specific situations presented.[4]

THE PRIMITIVE PREACHING

The primitive preaching [1] was that Jesus died for one's sins, was raised by God from among the dead, and was in heaven, where he would remain until the time appointed by God for the end of the age, when he would come as God's agent in the consummation of the age and the inauguration of the age to come.

It is evident that much of this had its origin in current apocalyptic and Jewish Scripture. It is equally plain that the general features correspond to the stories of dying and rising savior-gods common throughout the Near East and the Hellenistic world.

The evangelist uttered his message, full of conviction. Some of his hearers "believed." They gave evidence of their belief by uttering their "confession," e.g., "Jesus is [my] Lord," or, "Jesus Christ is Lord." The believers tended to congregate into little societies, so that "churches" [2] were formed. Baptism was a usual rite of entrance, and another sacrament, a communal meal in commemoration of the Lord's death, was observed.

These things meant to the believer that he was "saved." That is, his nature was changed or transformed: formerly he was lost, now he was saved. A variety of content was involved in these conceptions: one thought himself under control of evil demonic powers, subject to illness, suffering misfortune, destined to eternal punishment, by nature incapable of living rightly, rejected by the gods, and so forth. By believing, and as he believed, his life which had been under demonic control was now under the control of benign and holy spirit, the man became a new creature. Formerly fearful of what impended in the present life as well as in the afterlife, he was now confident of the good issue of present and future. Then, subject to disease, misfortune and death, now he expected health, welfare and a blissful eternal life.

Specific content differed among different people. Each thought in terms of familiar religious conceptions. In one case the dramatic representation of the mystery cult, in another the cosmic involvements of Jewish apocalyptic, in another theological interpretations of Jewish Scripture furnished source and pattern by which words expressed particular meaning.

But there were certain constants, also: one believed, he acknowledged belief in confession, and he was assured that thus he was "saved." It was usual for him to adhere to others of like experience, thus through baptism becoming a member of a church. To some extent he identified himself with others of the group in particular cult practices and ways of living.

The variables operated as different backgrounds obtained. If the believer came from the background of the Serapis cult, or with familiarity gained through initiation into the Eleusinian mystery, or from the training which one had in the complexities of the Roman religion, what he brought to his new experience largely conditioned his understanding of it. If he was a Jew his knowledge of Jewish lore, particularly of Scripture story, religious customs (e.g., dietary practices, household rituals, or Sabbath observance) and his customary moral code would likewise condition his apprehension of the new experience. Similarly, difference in content was occasioned by the location of believers and cults in the several territories of the ancient world.

Constants and variables may alike be illustrated [3] by some of Paul's observations. He mentions how the Thessalonians had "turned to God from idols, to serve a true and living God, and to wait for his Son from heaven, whom he raised from the dead: Jesus, who delivers us from the coming wrath" (1 Thess. 1:13). Obviously a number of these items were intellectualized interpretations of Jewish Scripture. On the other hand, the identification of Jesus as God's Son received gentile interpretations by many of his hearers and readers. Paul also drew upon Jewish apocalyptic expectations. He utilized, too, the familiar Jewish polemic against idolatry, and Jewish teaching about God's nature. Again he writes: "I delivered to you in the first place that which I received, namely, that Christ died for our sins according to the Scripture, and that he was buried, and that he was raised on the third day, also according to the Scripture, and that he appeared to Cephas, then to the twelve, then he appeared to more than five hundred brothers at the same time (of whom most still remain, although some are fallen asleep); then he appeared to James, then to all the apostles; last of all as to one born before his time he appeared to me." Tradition and Jewish interpretation are both used here.

The primitive preaching, it appears, was extremely simple. Adornment in detail, naturally leading to difference in content, was slight. It is also apparent that the messages were generally similar to Graeco-Roman cult stories and to apocalyptic messianism. The story readily lent itself to adaptation along these two lines. It was a simple matter for one to regard Jesus as a dying and rising savior-god, or for another to find him to be the Anointed who was expected to come on the clouds to bring into being the new heaven and earth.

The consequence of belief was more important than its content. It was of the greatest significance that believers came to have particular experiences, so that more or less characteristic ways of life developed in the religious groups. When one remembers that the believers included all sorts of people of divers localities, and that most [4] of them came into the fellowships in response to thoroughly individualistic impulses, it is remarkable that coherence and some working unity were ever achieved.

It is usually difficult for the modern student to accommodate himself to the emphasis upon Jesus' death which was made in the early preaching. But this he must do if he is to see what was the secret of its success. Undoubtedly the centrality of emphasis upon Jesus' death was due to the fact that what became Christianity began with the "resurrection" experiences. It was fortunate for the movement that the resurrection faith permitted obvious interpretations from the differing patterns of Jewish apocalyptic and the Hellenistic salvation cults. The basic emphasis upon Jesus' death was thoroughly congenial in both. The hearer of the story who was familiar with apocalyptic expectations naturally laid little emphasis upon the Messiah's earthly career, if, indeed, the thought occurred to him. Enough for him that Jesus had died and had been raised from among the dead and was in heaven whence he would one day come in his messianic capacity. Likewise the hearer who was familiar with the stories told in the salvation cults took for granted that the death, rather than the life, of the cult Lord was what effected salvation. In each case the central place accorded the death in the story of Jesus was natural, both for the teller and the hearer.

Emphasis upon Jesus' death in the primitive preaching carried an inevitable consequence. To the Jews the cross of Jesus was a stumbling block. Jesus had been executed as a criminal, and it was difficult for Jews to permit the amazing story of his rising from the dead to outweigh the importance of this fact. That an executed criminal, especially a crucified criminal, could be God's Anointed was extremely difficult for Jews to believe. In spite of the fact that those who had the " resurrection experiences " were Jews, in spite of the fact that the majority of their first hearers were Jews, it was exceptional for Jews to believe the stories. In spite of the ease with which the stories could be fitted into the schema of apocalyptic expectations, the response to the stories from Jewish hearers was not as readily favorable as was the response from non-Jews. The manner of Jesus' death was a factor in the negative response.

Conversely, the very emphasis upon Jesus' death in the preaching made it relatively easier for the non-Jew to entertain and believe it. He lacked the abhorrence of crucifixion which was a common Jewish attitude. The story of a savior who had been put to death by tragic evil was so familiar to him that the religious mind of the Hellenistic people may almost be said to have been predisposed toward it.

It is of importance, further, that the practice of drawing

upon Jewish Scripture to explain the story of Jesus led to the use of the familiar Greek translation. While Palestinian Jews did not use this translation, it must be remembered that Christianity early became current outside Palestine, and that the use of the Greek language in the primitive preaching naturally led to the use of the Greek version.

Who were the early Christian preachers? It is regrettable that this question can be answered in only the sketchiest way. Unless one contents oneself with the stories told in the early chapters of the Acts section of Luke-Acts he is reduced to the recital of the names supplied in the letters of Paul. One must treat the traditions of the Acts section as critically as it is necessary to treat the gospel section of Luke-Acts; the former as well as the latter is properly to be used as a witness to the period of its writing rather than as a witness to the period of its dramatic date. It is unnecessary to doubt that some of those mentioned in these traditions were historical persons, e.g., Barnabas. The correlation of Paul's notices with the traditions of the Acts section may perhaps be taken as a controlled statement: this would confirm statements about Peter, Barnabas and Apollos as particularly noteworthy. Paul particularly calls such persons as Timothy, Titus and Silvanus to attention. The list of names in what is now Romans 16 contains several whose bearers are cited as workers part of whose task may have been preaching. More names may be culled from the lists in his letters; indeed, the result of such a compilation is a fairly large number. A few seem to have been of some fame, as Andronicus and Junias, who are said to have been of note among the apostles and " in Christ " before Paul. Some, as Prisca and Aquila, and Philemon and Apphia, were also hosts and hostesses of house-churches. The place of women among these workers warrants attention.

But it would be a serious error to conclude that Paul's lists include all, or nearly all, of the early preachers. There were many who were outside Paul's circle. Who preached in places not visited by Paul? Whose messages had assembled the group in Damascus, all of whom were " in Christ " before Paul? Who evangelized Ephesus? Who first spoke in Rome? Who told of Jesus in Alexandria? Epaphras is said to have evangelized the Colossians. But naturally Paul's references to those outside his circle are few; his cordial statement about Apollos is quite exceptional. There can be no doubt that there were many preachers who were not only not associated with Paul, but whose work was conceived on quite different lines. The spread of the Christian movement in the few years which elapsed before Paul's advent is itself proof that there were effective leaders whose work, rather than whose names, was their memorial.

It is notable that among the leaders whose names have been perpetuated, Jesus' closest followers figure only slightly. Luke-Acts reports the tradition of the early death of James ben Zebedee, says much about Peter, and contains a few stories in which John figures. No other one of the so-called Twelve is reported as a worker in the emerging movement. To be sure, the Twelve is a sort of institution; its number is made complete, and it is said to have remained in Jerusalem during persecution, but, with the two exceptions noted, deeds of note are not related of its members. On the other hand, others, as James, Barnabas and Philip, not members of the institution, are said to have done far more than any member aside from Peter. Paul also mentions the Twelve, saying nothing of its individual members except Cephas and John. He, too, cites others as notable workers, e.g., Barnabas and Apollos, and mentions James with respect. It must be concluded that the twelve were not as important in the rise of Christianity as references to them in the gospels would lead one to expect. Late tradition ascribes heroic history to each one, but this was in the interest of hagiography, and has nothing to do with Christian beginnings.

One should not, of course, expect abundant information about the early Christian preachers. Their messages, not their names, were important. They told their stories; the realization of their purpose did not involve the establishment of their personal fame. To recognize the phenomenal success of their work, to appreciate the quick spread and distribution of Christianity as a result of their preaching, is adequate evidence that for the most part the stories of Jesus found effective messengers in sufficient number to insure the growth of Christianity.

PAUL

It is an interesting accident that only Paul is well known among the early preachers. When the statements of Luke-Acts are properly criticized they contribute but little concerning his life and work, but the information to be gleaned from his own letters is considerable. This is what distinguishes him from his contemporaries: there is a large and a highly important precipitate of his labors in what he wrote; there is no such witness to theirs.

Yet the stories about Paul in Luke-Acts and even the data of his letters have led to misunderstanding and have created problems. More abundant literary attestation has warped the common perspective, and has led to the mistaken judgment that Paul was not only the greatest exponent of the primitive preaching, but that he was the founder of the gentile mission. The former estimate is gratuitous, in view of lack of information concerning others; the latter judgment is plainly wrong. Abundant information about Paul and lack of it about others has similarly caused the currency of the erroneous notion that early Christianity, wherever found, was the same as the religion of the Pauline communities.

Paul was one of a fairly large number of exponents of the story of Jesus. He was frank to credit others with the distinctions and results due them. He observed that others were "in Christ" before him and pointed out that others were "energized" for work whose importance he would have been the last to depreciate. When he differed from other messengers he admitted their right to their work and in certain cases related his work to theirs: Apollos watered what he planted and God blessed the labors of both. He recognized the propriety of an opponent's position: he was entirely cordial to James, although he saw that his position and James's were antithetical. When a difference between himself and Cephas became acute he argued it, recognizing Cephas' place in religious work.

Paul was not the founder of the policy of taking the story of Jesus to non-Jews. The older impression probably results from reading the stories of Luke-Acts uncritically. A careful study relieves it of the responsibility for this misapprehension. Luke-Acts tells that Paul came into contact with members of the cult of Jesus some time after the inception of the movement. Indeed, according to Luke-Acts, Paul's activity as a "persecutor" was intended to be applied in the region of Damascus — the emerging Christian movement had, then, reached so distant an outpost before Paul's "conversion." In another narrative it is related that Paul found disciples in Ephesus: the implication is obvious. To the same effect is the datum that Paul found "brothers" when he arrived in Rome; his letter corroborates the fact that Christianity was in Rome independently of and before him. Luke-Acts also implies [1] the currency of Christianity in Alexandria: this, too, was independent of Paul.

Paul's letters also assume the existence of cults of Jesus before and independent of his own work. The bearing of his letter to Rome has been pointed out. The letter to the

Colossians, whether by Paul or not, was to a church not founded by him. Indeed, Paul explicitly states that he avoided " building upon the foundation which another had laid." He refers to Peter's work with Jews, speaks of the Jerusalem group, and more than once mentions the Judean churches. Thus while it is a fortunate accident that primary sources furnish a wealth of information about Paul's work, it must not be assumed that his was the sole nor the major work of the early days, nor that his achievements were normative for others.

Paul is the more interesting because he is an example of those early Christian leaders who were Jewish. He was, to be sure, one who lived outside Palestine,[2] and his Judaism was affected by his contact with gentile culture, especially by the influence of the Greek language. Yet Paul affirms that his life was strictly Jewish, that he was brought up according to strict Pharisaic standards, and that his life according to this standard had been exemplary. With such modifications as were required by residence in the gentile locality Paul was taught Jewish lore on the basis of Scripture and Torah.

The apocalyptic element in Paul's religion raises questions. Under the influence of R. H. Charles it used to be commonly thought that the apocalypses represented typical Judaism.[3] But when the work of Herford, Abrahams, Dibelius and Moore popularized information about legalistic Judaism [4] this view was challenged. Apocalyptic was shown to be an eddy aside from the main stream of Judaism, which was legalistic and similar to that which later was articulated in the rabbinical writings.

Certainly Paul made important use of apocalyptic in his

religious life and teaching. It greatly facilitated his identification of Jesus as Anointed, and gave concrete form to his beliefs about the sort of Anointed Jesus was (and was to be). It centrally affected his world-view, doing much to formulate his judgments of the nature of the world and of its cosmic future. It led him to several detailed and specific judgments, e.g., what might otherwise be considered as asceticism was probably significant of his vivid expectation of the end of the age; also, his judgment that marriage was impracticable. Apocalyptic influenced his attitude toward the State.

Was Paul as avidly apocalyptic in his earlier life as he was after his experience of Jesus? No answer to this is possible, no guess has value. One may, however, remark that since scholars have demonstrated the normative character of legalistic Judaism the apocalyptic element in Paul marks him as untypical of Judaism in this respect. Difference from Palestinian norms also obtained as a result of Paul's life in the world of the dispersion Jew.

It must be remembered that Paul's references to his earlier religious life are all made later and on the basis of his new and revolutionary experience. It is impossible to take his remarks about his former experience as purely objective. For example, he once says that according to the standard of Torah he was blameless. But on another occasion he reports a case typically as though it were his own, saying that Torah had had a thoroughly unfortunate effect, and that consciousness of sin followed the attempt to practice the pattern of the Law. Clearly Paul's later experience strongly influenced his estimates of his earlier life.

To be sure, that Paul's first reaction to the story of Jesus was thoroughly negative indicates his sincere loyalty to Judaism. He says that he was impelled to oppose the emerging Christian movement to the point of persecution. This emphasizes his devotion. It proves that in Paul Judaism had a loyal and an enthusiastic representative. This is supported by every relevant consideration in Paul's remarks about his earlier life.

Other inferences are often made. The tradition that Paul studied for the rabbinate in Jerusalem is as old as Luke-Acts. Since the "life of Paul" is usually a weaving together of the data of Luke-Acts, information from the letters and other traditions, several examples of rabbinical exegesis and theology are conveniently found to prove that Paul was a trained rabbi. However, serious doubt is thrown upon the assertion when the primary sources are critically studied.[5] In this matter, as in others, a negative attitude should be taken to a tradition which owes its currency to tendentious elements in Luke-Acts. Other details, largely drawn or inferred from Luke-Acts, should be similarly judged, e.g., that Paul was a member of " the Sanhedrin " (it would be necessary to inquire, which Sanhedrin?), that he was involved in the death of Stephen, and was, indeed, a persecutor of far greater ferocity than his own self-reproachful words would indicate. A candid generalization should include only what was suggested above, that Paul in his earlier life was a loyal, if not a typical, legalistic Jew.

The new and revolutionary phase in Paul's religious life came as a quite extraordinary experience. He had heard the propaganda about Jesus, and had taken a strongly negative attitude toward it. His devotion to Judaism as he knew it was such that he felt obliged to oppose the new movement, even to persecute its exponents. But the astounding event occurred: he "saw" Jesus. He concluded that God had given him a revelation. He generalized, at least as he stated it later, that God had revealed his Son in him, and had set him apart for a work which was itself part of God's plan.

While it is impossible to derive from Paul's statements any large content which can be scientifically controlled, it is inviting to view his experience as one of the whole number of those persons who "saw" Jesus. Paul recounts it as the final one of a series which began with Cephas and included several others. If theirs were to be understood as Paul explained his, the basis of the primitive preaching might be stated with greater confidence. The point is important when it is remembered that the resurrection stories of the gospels are much later than Paul's references to his experience of the risen Jesus, and that their apparent objectivity is largely due to the fixity which these stories assumed in their repetition. One must regard Paul's statements about his experience as the primary source for the study of the beginning of the resurrection stories.

It is another modernizing misconception to call Paul's experience a "conversion." There is no reason so to regard it. He was not converted from something to something else. He never abandoned Judaism, nor does he seem to have regarded his new life as in any sense separated from Judaism. He understood his experience as transforming his nature. It made a new man of the former man. As a considerably later rationalization he insisted that the experience did for him what Torah could not do: it secured for him the status of "not guilty" in the judgment of God. But the aid which he found in Scripture in understanding his experience the more emphasizes the fact that it was not un-Jewish as he saw it. Indeed, it is possible to point to the " Jewish bias " [6] of Paul. It may be apparent to moderns that Paul's work had the effect of working a cleavage between the growing cults of Jesus and Judaism, but it was not apparent to Paul.

Paul later made a theological explanation of his experience, and then, with the same enthusiasm as that with which he had opposed Christianity, he began to propagate it. He became an evangelist of the faith which he had opposed and persecuted.

Paul propagated a certain type of the religious life, a type which was to some extent exemplified by members of the communities which he founded. He did this by making his own experience the norm for others. Not that they were expected to " see " Jesus; that part of his experience was exceptional. But they were expected to respond to his recital of it, and to accept his interpretation of it: they were expected to believe that Jesus had died for their sins, that God raised him from among the dead, that he was in heaven, whence he will come when God's anger breaks out against a wicked age. Belief in these items of the story of Jesus and confession of him as Lord secured for the believer the status of " not guilty " before God's judgment. He was saved; his nature was transformed; from being evil he was good, the old was new, the flesh-person was now spirit-person.

Spirit was indeed an important element in the religious life as Paul conceived it. When one believed, holy spirit took its abode in him and manifested its presence in different ways. Evidently the most usual expression was that of causing the believer to speak in unintelligible gibberish: " speaking in a tongue," or glossolalia, to use Paul's word. Some of Paul's disciples were excessively fond of this. Paul valued much higher the spirit's prompting a prophetic message. Sometimes spirit caused one to heal the sick, in other cases it expressed itself in ability to teach or to do something in the government of a church. There was much variety, even confusion, in the way spirit expressed itself in the Pauline groups. Probably this is a point of difference between Pauline and non-Pauline churches: spiritistic behavior was congenial to and characteristic of Paul and the people of his churches, while it was much less so in communities founded and guided by other leaders.

Paul emphasized that God had commissioned him to carry his message to non-Jews. He remarked that God had likewise commissioned Peter to work among Jews, and he seems to have taken it for granted that James and John rightfully worked in their spheres. But for him the important item was the commission to go to the non-Jews. This is what he did. He says that he worked for seventeen years in Syria and Cilicia, making certain visits to Jerusalem. Aside from these facts nothing is known of his activity before he wrote his letters.

Paul's evangelization of non-Jews brought to the fore an important question, the answer to which he consistently and constantly asserted. The question was whether non-Jews upon believing must become circumcised, i.e., join the Jewish people. Paul insisted that he always and successfully maintained that they need not and that they must not.

That he should have taken this position may at first seem surprising. He was a devoted Jew. He never ceased to value Judaism nor to insist upon the advantage of being a Jew. It is highly probable that Paul's spiritism led him to this position: since gentile believers manifested spirit possession as did Jews he concluded that the belief which caused Jew and non-Jew to become spirit-filled secured the status of " not guilty," hence it was not only not necessary for the non-Jew to become a Jew, but for him to do so would entail the loss of his status as a guiltless spirit-person.

Further, that the believer must not become a Jew was maintained by Paul on the ground that anyone might believe, whether the believer were Jew or non-Jew, Greek or non-Greek, man or woman, slave or free.　Since belief transformed one's nature, belief (or, to use the more familiar term, faith) did what observing Torah had not done for Paul.　He went so far as to say that observance of Torah had never done this for anyone; indeed, that it could not do it for anyone.　Paul thus distinguished between two ways of the religious life, and he affirmed that the faith-way was the only valid one.　The Jew had a certain advantage, chiefly in possessing Scripture, but the non-Jew need not and must not become a Jew.

In this Paul was making use of the individualism which was so characteristic of the Hellenistic age.[7]　That it would result in bringing into being religious societies which would become serious rivals of Judaism seems never to have been seen by Paul.　That he made use of this attitude is understandable in view of his being a Hellenistic, rather than a Palestinian Jew.　Probably other exponents of the primitive preaching used it; it will be remembered that preaching to non-Jews had been practiced some time before Paul became a teller of the story of Jesus.　It has been well said that Paul is a product of gentile Christianity.[8]

One of Paul's most vigorous affirmations is that he never deviated from the message which he had preached in the years before he wrote his letters. After the seventeen years of this activity he went on several [9] journeys to the West, evangelizing a number of communities and founding societies, to some of which he wrote his letters. In these letters the essential characteristics of the Pauline type of religious life may be observed. From them nothing contradicts his statement that he represented these principles.

However, it should be kept in mind that the message of Paul is only incidentally derivable from the letters. His work was to preach, and this he did. His achievements were realized through the spoken word, not through writing. It is erroneous to use the letters to derive from them a theological system; it is wrong to conclude that his message is fully found in them. He wrote to deal with particular matters; only occasionally is a statement of his message made.

Paul visited more places than those referred to in his letters; he founded more societies than those to whom he wrote. He worked according to plan: avoiding competition with other leaders, he attempted to cover as thoroughly as possible the territories of the north Mediterranean coast. He worked westward, contemplating a visit to Rome en route to Spain. Why did he not envisage work in Alexandria?

At all events, he planted cults of Jesus in a number of centers of the Empire. The movement which he introduced there lived after him. It developed in ways not traceable to his influence, and in ways of which he would probably have disapproved. Yet these places were of prime importance in the Romanization of the East, so that his work related to the development of Hellenistic culture in his period.

The achievement of a proper perspective will afford the

perception that Paul was a great leader and that his work was of major importance, but it will also show that he propagated a type of the religious life which was not universally characteristic of the Christian movement. It will also require the recognition that in the East, the South, and the farther North others were achieving results which, like his, were of permanent significance.

IV

THE EARLIEST EXTANT CHRISTIAN WRITING

As was noted, Paul's letters were incidental and adventitious results of his work as a messenger of the story of Jesus. They were written late in his work. The extant letters represent but a fraction of his activity; they do not account for all his writing. While it is idle to speculate whether Paul wrote anything previous to his earliest extant letter, it is true that he wrote at least one letter which was not preserved. Of other letters the present forms are but fragments of the originals. It is probable that all surviving letters have undergone considerable editorial modification.

Paul's extant letters include documents addressed to only a few of the churches which he founded. Since these discuss particular problems of specific situations it is manifestly improper to derive from them generalized articulations of a unified picture of "Christianity," or even of "Pauline Christianity." The individual situation must always be kept in mind.

It was only after Paul had taken the story of Jesus from the continent of Asia to the continent of Europe that the impulse to write occurred to him. This, at any rate, is the significant implication of the usually accepted sequence of the letters.[1] According to this consensus, the first[2] letter was written to people in Thessalonica, people whom Paul had evangelized with enough success to bring together a society of believers, only to have trouble develop. He had to leave the city. Yet he found that the people were much on his mind; although he was confident of their sincerity he was so concerned about their fate that he sent Timothy, one of his associates, from Athens to Thessalonica to inquire about them. After receiving Timothy's report he wrote what is known as First Thessalonians.

Writing with Silvanus and Timothy, Paul warmly commends the Thessalonian believers. He recounts aspects of his work with them and in their neighborhood, especially noting the difficulties encountered, and discloses his anxieties on their behalf. He expresses his joyous relief on learning that they had survived the critical difficulties of their first days as believers. He exhorts them to live moral lives. He instructs them about details of the imminent end of the age, particularly assuring them that believers who died before the end would not be at a loss as against those living at the time.

The letter plainly exhibits characteristics of Paul's type of the religious life. The Thessalonians were accustomed to ecstatic seizures; since Paul urges them not to stifle the spirit it may be inferred, however, that some deprecated this type of experience. Paul remarks that it was unnecessary to tell them about the end of the age; obviously they had accepted his vivid apocalypticism. The moral exhortations show that there was not in every case the union of spiritism and behavior which was desired in Paul's code.

This brings to light a problem which often appeared. When persons responded to Paul's highly spiritistic preaching, some brought into the newly founded cults of Jesus the moral patterns to which they were habituated; sometimes these patterns left much to be desired, from Paul's viewpoint. It must be borne in mind that there was as yet no Christian moral pattern — this had yet to be achieved. Paul, like many moralists, assumed that believers would adopt the code to which he was accustomed to conform, but they did not always do so. But he was confident that the Thessalonians would readily adjust their moral to their spiritistic living.

Paul found it necessary to urge the Thessalonians to respect their religious leaders; evidently this was a problem. Perhaps the depreciation of spiritism and prophesying created it; doubtless the leaders who remained when Paul left were ardent spiritists like Paul himself, while others in the church who placed less emphasis upon this feature of the religious life differed in this respect.

The authenticity of Second Thessalonians has been frequently questioned. The basis of doubt is the alleged difference from the normal Pauline apocalyptic expectation; the letter tends to negative the immediacy of the expected end of the age, basing the postponement upon a theory that there is a temporary restraining force, as well as certain processes and instruments in the program of the end.

However, there are details in the letter which admirably fit the Thessalonian situation, thus authenticating it as a sort of sequel to the former. For example, the second letter intimates that erroneous views have been propagated as Paul's by means of forged letters, so that Paul here indicates his custom of writing the subscription of genuine letters in his own hand.

Again, this source pictures believers who so vividly expect the end of the age that they have stopped working to

await it. It was consonant with the Pauline emphasis both
that they should do so, and that he should lay down the principle that idlers were not to be supported.

Paul's letter to the Galatians [8] was written to several communities in " Galatia " which Paul had evangelized at some
earlier time. The character and purpose of the letter are
apparent. The situation was serious. The people who had
believed Paul's message and had formed churches had afterward listened to propagandists who had affirmed that the
believers must accept circumcision (thus joining the Jewish
people) and become amenable to all requirements of Torah.
They were impressed and persuaded; they had already be-
gun to observe sabbaths and were at the point of accepting
the obligation to become circumcised. Paul wrote in the heat
of passion, defending the validity of his message and insisting that the Galatians must not do what these leaders had
urged.

The opponents had intimated that Paul's authority and
message were of questionable validity; inasmuch as he had
not been a follower of Jesus he must have obtained his message from secondary sources. Paul insists that it came directly from God: God revealed his Son in him. This is
quite consonant with the radical spiritism of Paul; is it
possible that the " fourteen years " of Galatians 2:1 and 2
Corinthians 12:2 give a clew to the experience in which the
" revelation " was given? Only on rare occasions, Paul says,
did he visit Jerusalem and meet other leaders, Cephas, James
and John. Even then he acquired nothing from them of content of his message.

This information heightens the necessary impression of
the individuality of the Pauline type of religion. On one

occasion, it is said, Paul went to Jerusalem — " by revelation " — to discuss his missionary methods with other leaders. The question was whether it was proper to receive non-Jews as believers without requiring them to become Jews (this is the ultimate meaning of the demand that they be circumcised). Paul reports that his consistent practice was endorsed; this in spite of certain " false brothers " who were " smuggled in " to force a different policy. The outcome was that Paul was to continue evangelizing non-Jews, while Peter worked among Jews.

Paul tells of a sharp difference between himself and Cephas [4] in Antioch. It had been the custom of Cephas, as of Paul and others, to have inclusive fellowship with non-Jews in the Antiochene community, but when representatives of James came from Jerusalem to Antioch, Cephas and Barnabas changed their way. Paul remonstrated with Cephas. His reasoning was that since Cephas owed his religious status to his faith-experience,[5] and since in line with this he had been living with others who had also been pronounced acquitted [6] by their faith, it was hypocritically inconsistent now to live on the basis of Jewish custom and to compel non-Jews to do the same. This example led Paul to articulate the principle upon which his whole " gospel " was based: no one is pronounced acquitted by doing what Torah requires; one is pronounced acquitted by his belief in the story of Jesus. Further, everyone who exercises that faith, whether he be Jew or non-Jew, is thereby pronounced acquitted.

Paul proceeds to argue this principle in detail. He is not highly effective in argument. His assertions depend upon a thoroughly arbitrary and mechanical use of Scripture, so that it is made to teach, not its intended meaning, but the meaning which Paul wishes it to teach. That "Abraham believed God" and that "his belief was credited to him as justness" proves for Paul the validity of the faith experience for his own believers. That a promise was made to Abraham's "seed" enables Paul to base an argument on the singular number of the word, and, in spite of the plain fact that the promise meant something entirely different, to affirm that by the "seed" Jesus was meant.

Paul uses figures of speech somewhat more effectively: Torah (or, rather, the Law,[7] as he prefers to call it) once had a certain validity which it no longer possesses; it was for mankind what the paedagogue was to the Greek child, the slave who conducted him to his teacher — the Law was the slave who brought the believer to Jesus. The slave figure was used further: a child is hardly better in legal status than a slave; we used to be slaves to the cosmic elements,[8] but God sent his Son to redeem us from this slavery — to adopt Judaism would be to reinstitute slavery. Again, the two conditions might be compared to two Abrahamic covenants, leading to two lines of descent, one from Hagar the slave, one from the freewoman, Sarah. By the use of the allegorical method, long familiar in Greek literary tradition, Paul makes these two covenants represent Mount Sinai (where Torah was first given, corresponding to Jerusalem) and the Jerusalem which is above, the type of freedom; believers are therefore children of the free woman and of the free Jerusalem. This is devious reasoning, but characteristic of the teacher who had convenient methods of making Scripture mean what he wished it to mean.

In direct argument and exhortation Paul insists that if any

believer accepts circumcision he forfeits his status in Christ and is obliged to keep the entire Torah; one who expects to be pronounced acquitted through law cannot hope to enjoy the status which is God's gift. Paul is extremely irritated; the Galatians were doing excellently when they were subverted. In his rancor Paul expresses the wish that they who were inducing the Galatians to cut off the foreskin would from themselves cut off the penis.

As in the Thessalonian situation, Paul found it necessary to urge that the spirit life must not become a life of license;[9] believers must live moral lives.

No letter of Paul's is easier to understand than Galatians. Yet it presents difficult questions. Did the opposing leaders represent Judaism, or a cult of Jesus which maintained that all disciples must observe Torah; were they Jews or Jewish-Christians?[10] When it is remembered that to adopt circumcision as the primary element of Judaism means that the candidate was thus joining the Jewish people and race, the logical propriety in regarding these persons as Jewish-Christians is dissipated. There was no half-Jewish, half-Christian status. The person who identified Jesus as Anointed and insisted that Jewish Torah must be observed was not a Jewish-Christian, but a Jew. On the other hand, for a Jew to believe that Jesus was Anointed did not make him less a Jew. It follows that Paul's opponents in Galatia were Jews whose opposition was legitimate Jewish propaganda. They are witnesses of the spread of Judaism in the far reaches of the world.

The arguments in Galatians imply another trend. Even more plainly than in the Thessalonian letter, or letters, there is evidence of persons who acted upon a logical implication of Paul's spiritism. They held that when they exercised faith and became spirit-persons the spirit life was superior to and independent of the flesh life. They acted upon this principle, and behaved accordingly, becoming complete antinomians.[11] Naturally, this was quite incompatible with any current moral code. Evidence of such disciples of Paul is to be found in other letters; [12] persons of this type of experience were present in several of his communities. Toward them Paul took a practical, albeit an illogical, position: spirit-persons must live according to a conventional moral code.[13]

Paul had a full correspondence with the members of the church in Corinth. He had evangelized the Corinthians after having been forced to leave Thessalonica, and was later working in Ephesus. He wrote a letter (mentioned in 1 Cor. 5:9) the main point of which was a warning not to associate with immoral people. The Corinthians, or some of them, wrote a letter to him, asking certain questions. The letter known as First Corinthians is in part a reply to this letter.

" First " Corinthians reveals several disturbing elements in this community. The church had developed factions, with a party devoted to the leadership of Cephas, of Apollos and of Paul. Church people had disputes which they took to civil (and therefore pagan) courts. There was flagrant sexual immorality, including a case which Paul insisted was incestuous. Certain church ordinances were scandalously held; the Lord's Supper was an occasion of gluttony and drunkenness. Paul disapproved of women's taking part in the services. Expressions of spirit possession were uncontrolled, with too great emphasis upon the less important of them. Since some were puzzled about certain religious questions, e.g., how life after death was to be lived bodily, or whether it was proper to eat food which had been sacrificially slaughtered, Paul gave instruction on these points. Some were doubtful whether they should marry, and some married people wondered whether they should separate from their partners.

The problems and their answers give much information about an early "Christian" community. For instance, the Corinthian group may be taken as a fair sample of the proletarian life of the ancient world. "Not many wise people, not many powerful people, not many of the well-born" were in the group (1:26). The cult members were ordinary low class persons who had responded to Paul's message of individual redemption. They represented converts from the seamy side of paganism; Paul once refers to sexually immoral persons, idolaters, adulterers, effeminate (in the obscene sense) persons, sexual perverts, thieves, people guilty of excess, drunkards, revilers and extortioners, and adds that "some of you were such as these" (6:11).

The Corinthians avidly responded to the spiritistic impulses which accompanied their religious lives. But in some respects they were recalcitrant, stubborn and self-willed. While Paul regarded himself as their parent in the religious life, some of them, responding to other leaders, rebelled against him. In spite of his instruction that they narrow to a minimum their contacts with grossly immoral outsiders, some of them not only condoned immorality, but kept a certain offender in standing in the church.

Others were unduly ascetic. Some took the position that marriage was incompatible with the spirit life; hence they must sever their marital relationships. Some had decided to refrain from sexual experience with their partners. Some had determined not to marry, so as to devote themselves utterly to the religious life.

Contrasting with these, there were still others who reacted so radically to Paul's emphasis upon freedom that they became libertines.

In meeting their problems, Paul deprecates their factions. He observed that Cephas and Apollos, as well as he, were doing God's work. He points out that his preaching was deliberately in utter simplicity, thus any lack of human wisdom in his message was no sign of his inferiority nor of their superiority; on the contrary, each worked in his own way and God blessed the result. Paul sternly offers the people an alternative: he expects to come to them soon, and inquires whether he shall come in authority (literally, " with a club ") or gently. He insists upon strict standards of morality, directing that there should be no social fellowship with immoral people. Likewise he required that differences between cult members be settled privately, without recourse to civil courts.

In answering the questions which they had asked, Paul first took up the matter of marriage. He stated the advantages of the single life in a way which suggests that he saw little value in marriage beyond the controlled expression of sexual impulses. However, he recommended that married persons should remain so, and cautioned them against protracted inhibition of sexual relationship. Although he taught that the single life was practically better, he advised marriage for those whose sexual inclinations were very strong.[14]

About eating food which had been slaughtered in idolatrous ritual, Paul took a practical position. The fact of sacrificial offering had not affected the food, which might be eaten with impunity. But if some sensitive person should raise a question about the propriety of eating it, consideration for his point of view should lead one to refrain from its use.

In these matters it is easy to see that membership in a cult of Jesus had not necessarily led to a complete change in the believer's way of life. Some, at least, did not discontinue frequenting pagan temples (8:10). Common beliefs appear: Paul, who denied any divinity in an idol, affirmed that back of the idol was a demon (10:20–22). This was the basis of his rule that one might not participate in pagan ceremonies; one might not share in the table and the cup of the Lord (Jesus) and the table and cup of demons.

Paul's statements about himself are instructive. The principle of expediency is illustrated by his citing several rules which he might have, but had not, followed, as taking pay for his work, or being accompanied by a wife (as were the other apostles, Jesus' brothers and Cephas). He makes the famous statement that he became all things to all men. In doing so his figures betray the degree to which he was influenced by Hellenistic life; his figures include reference to the gymnasium, the stadium, and racing and boxing (9:24–27).

Not less instructive are the discussions of cult practices. Although the Corinthians remember him and " hold fast the traditions " (11:2) there are some unsatisfactory conditions. The women have taken too much authority; they participate in cult services, praying and speaking with bared head. They must subordinate themselves to the men, Paul says, and under no circumstances appear uncovered in public. This teaching has caused much concern to moderns. Is Paul here utterly reactionary, maintaining current social attitudes which assumed woman's inferiority? It should not be expected that Paul would differ radically from current conventions, were it not that his spiritism elsewhere (Galatians 3:28) led him to enunciate the principle that in Christ sexual as well as racial and social distinctions are obliterated; clearly this principle is contradicted here. It is clear, also, that Paul is motivated by a superstitious world view; his reason why a woman should be under authority is "because of the angels."

The bad manners of the Corinthians in the Lord's Supper gave Paul so much concern that he discusses the proper manner of its observance in some detail. In so doing he states information of great value. Indeed, he quotes the primitive ritual. Again, the emphasis upon tradition is significant; Paul passed on to them what he had received from the Lord. In this tradition the Supper was clearly a memorial, but it is equally clear that in making his own interpretations Paul largely conforms to elements of the contemporary world view; the sacramental aspects of the Supper are plain. There is something almost magical in his conception of the spiritistic power of the sacrament — improper observance of it has caused some of the Corinthians to fall victim of disease and death.

First Corinthians 12–14 is the *locus classicus* of information on early Christian spiritism. Much is to be learned from the passage. Even though the Corinthians were unusually spiritistic as compared with other Pauline Christians, it is certain that spiritism characterized many of the early disciples. In this instance behavior in spirit possession sometimes got out of control, and in some cases it was (Paul believed) the result of possession by the wrong spirit. Sometimes the spirit-filled person said, " Cursed be Jesus "; such a man was possessed by evil spirit, for one filled by holy spirit might be expected to say, " Jesus is Lord."

The major problem, however, was that the Corinthians generally had a faulty set of values in respect to spirit manifestation. Spirit-filled people did a number of different things. Some uttered prophecies, some gave messages of teaching, some did works of healing, others worked other types of mighty deeds, while still others " spoke in a tongue " or were inspired to interpret such speaking. Too many, in Paul's view, were expressing themselves in these glossolalia. As a result, their meetings were disorderly, with a number of people speaking unintelligibly at the same time. Outsiders must think them insane. In any case edification of the group was hindered. Paul pointed out that all these types of experience were the result of possession by holy spirit. He remarked that " I speak in a tongue more than all of you," and he urged them to speak thus, but he insisted that other expressions of spirit life were of superior value. He rated the entire range, placing prophecy first and glossolalia last. He urged practical considerations, e.g., that glossolalia were not understood (unless someone was inspired to interpret), which meant that the group was not instructed as it would be by superior manifestations; that it was impossible for the company to make the proper ritual response, and the effect upon non-members was bad.

Paul's ideal pattern (14:26–40) is of great interest. Members should contribute to common worship and instruction; one will sing a psalm, one will offer a teaching, one will impart a revelation which he has had, one will speak in a tongue a message which another will interpret. More than one, but not more than three, may speak in a tongue; but if no one present interprets no one is to speak in a tongue in common meeting. Two or three prophetic messages will be offered and interpreted. If another is inspired to speak the present speaker must give way to him. Women are not to speak at all. All should hope to be inspired to prophesy, but glossolalia are not to be forbidden. The meeting was partly ritualistic, as is shown by the fact that people must know when to pronounce the Amen.

Ecstatic behavior was common in Pauline Christianity. It was highly valued by Paul and by his church members. These phenomena characterized a considerable proportion of the members of the cults of Jesus in this early period. They were central in Paul's religion. This largely explains the subordinate place of teaching of Jesus in Paul's letters (and, probably, in his preaching). Likewise his use of Scripture only for evidential purpose is explained; Romans 12 is readily understood in the light of its implied appeal to give freer expression to the charismata.

The closing messages of 1 Corinthians are didactic and practical. Considerable space is given exposition of resurrection as a true and an important teaching. Indeed, it is part of the "tradition." The list of traditional "resurrection appearances," the first being to Cephas, the last to Paul, and the meaningful distinction between "the twelve" and "all the apostles" (incidentally, the primitivity of this reference to the twelve) [15] are important data in the study of early Christianity. One will not overlook the importance of Paul's citation of the appearance of Jesus to himself in the whole sequence of resurrection appearances, implying, as it does, that the several "appearances" were similar in nature.

Likewise Paul's classification of himself as an apostle is significant, and his mention of himself as a persecutor is more so.

The section has for its main subject the question of the resurrection from among the dead. It is discussed in the light of the tradition about Jesus' resurrection. To Paul this was of primary importance; Jesus' resurrection, accepted without question, guaranteed the resurrection of the believer. As Paul saw it, the ultimate consequence of Jesus' resurrection is cosmic; in his triumph over death Jesus reduced everything, including death, to subjection. This explains why, as Paul notes, people are baptized by proxy, so that those who had died previously may share the cosmic benefits. It also explains why Paul lived as he did — the hope of resurrection was for him a powerful sanction.

In details of resurrection faith Paul habitually thought in Jewish terms, while his hearers naturally thought in Greek terms. It was natural for a Jew to contemplate the resurrection life in terms of life with a body, but this was incomprehensible to the Greek; to him life after death in or with a body was a contradiction in terms. Paul had to explain to such people how it was that the dead arose, and how they were equipped with a body. His explanation was that there were different kinds of body, a flesh, a " psychic " and a spirit body; the resurrection would be with a spirit body. It is not known how convincing this explanation was to the Greek-thinking Corinthians.

Very practical details of instruction to contribute money weekly reflect further information about the cult life of the Corinthians. They are told to value leaders and to discover others like those specifically named by Paul. Paul's own paragraph of subscription includes a curse upon those who have no love for the Lord and an ejaculated prayer (in Aramaic) that the Lord come quickly.

As has been pointed out, "First" Corinthians is the second letter which Paul wrote to the people of Corinth. Critical study of the remaining elements of the Corinthian correspondence [16] has led to the inference, now widely accepted, that 2 Corinthians 10–13 is a fragment of Paul's next letter, written in a tone which was occasioned by the fact that 1 Corinthians failed in its objective. So far from correcting the abuses to which it addressed itself, the hostility to Paul was intensified to the point where it was a critical issue whether he could maintain his authority. The obvious emotional relief expressed in 2 Corinthians 1–9 suggests that this is the final part of the extant correspondence, and that the severe letter to which it refers (7:8) — 2 Corinthians 10–13 — had won its point.

No one will affirm that this now conventional reconstruction of the sequence of the Corinthian correspondence can be proved. But it corresponds with successive situations. For example, the contrast of the irony and rancor of 2 Corinthians 10–13 and the warm ardor of 1–9 suits the hypothesis perfectly. Thus viewed, all of 2 Corinthians is a most valuable source for the study of Paul's personality. Ardent, violent, ecstatic, emotionally unstable — Paul appears as thoroughly human. The composite letter also reveals much of Paul's expectations of the people. The religion which is normative is one of high, vivid spirituality; emotional satisfactions are much more obvious than intellectual content.

The fragment of the harsh letter is no less instructive. It contains, for example, the list of sufferings and persecution experiences (11:22–33) which give far more information about Paul's life than is furnished by Luke-Acts. Again, the ecstatic experience referred to in 12:1–18 is extraordinarily revealing. This passage is usually understood as picturing an experience of Paul himself. It goes far to illustrate Paul's religion as an ardent apocalyptist. It is possible that the reference to " fourteen years ago " should be considered together with the similar statistic of Galatians 2:1, 2. If so, the experience was of fundamental importance in Paul's life; it was a particular aspect of his vision of Paradise that it included God's revelation of his Son.

Finally, Paul's insistence that he is not to be regarded as inferior to the other apostles is significant, especially in the pragmatic way in which the argument is put: the people had had the signs of an apostle demonstrated in Paul's marvelous acts.

It is the value of the hypothesis that this sequence enables the student to observe the development and the issue of difficult and strained situations. Paul was dogmatic and arbitrary in his expectations of his people. He managed them with a high hand. He made his own type of experience normative for them. Not always consistent in his reasons for his requirements, he was always insistent that what he thought proper must be done. He was particularly inconsistent in his ethical requirements. On the one hand he stressed the imminence of the end of the age, and emphasized the impelling force of spirit. On the other hand he maintained conventional standards of morality and required the people to conform to them. There has been much speculation about the sources of Paul's ethic,[17] but the one fact which stands out clearly is that his primary ethical motivation was his spiritism.[18] Some of his contemporaries thought much more logically and consistently than he did, and saw that if one was a spirit-person the fact determined his nature and his ethical status. Some drew from this the inference which Paul repudiated with abhorrence; doubtless others accepted his word for what the practical life of spirit entailed in practice. At all events, the Corinthian correspondence is a valuable source for the study of the religious life of Paul and of some of his people.

Paul's letter " to the Romans " [19] has striking differences from the others. Its tone lacks vividness. It is cool and reasoned. Its thought proceeds from point to point as the development of the argument requires. Again, it differs in Paul's relation to its situation. He had never visited Rome. The church had been founded by someone else, and Paul was not accustomed to address churches founded by others. Naturally he was unable to make the personal references usually characteristic of his letters.

However, although he had never visited Rome, Paul had often thought of going there. He would have liked to make the journey as he wrote. But the collection for the relief of the members of the Jerusalem group had become the determining factor; his plan was made to go to the East with the offering. He was probably in Corinth when he wrote. This strikingly dramatizes the situation. For with equal facility he might have embarked upon a westbound or an eastbound ship. Electing to go eastward, he wrote the letter instead of making the visit. He was under no illusion about the probable reception in Jerusalem, for he requested his readers to " agonize " with him in prayer that he might escape from those in Judea who were disobedient. Nevertheless he was determined to go. He wrote the letter, as he says, " to exchange some charismatic gift " with the recipients.

Romans first presents Paul's convictions about how God pronounces men acquitted. He does it as and when they exercise faith, i.e., when they believe that God raised Jesus from among the dead and when they confess him to be Lord. God does this, then, because of his own nature and because of the nature of men. God is just. But the world presents a sorry picture. For men, capable of knowing the nature of God, have attended, rather, to unprofitable speculations, and morally they are utterly base. In this situation everyone is responsible, whether he be Jew or non-Jew. The Jew developed Law and is responsible to obey it; the non-Jew is also responsible, since he has standards which approximate the requirements of Law. But although everyone is responsible, there is no hope that anyone can meet his responsibility. True, the Jew has a primary advantage, since God revealed himself in (Jewish) Scripture. But in his reliance upon Law the Jew has placed his trust in the wrong place, for the most that the Law can do is to articulate a consciousness of sin. The Jew cannot be pronounced acquitted by keeping the Law, nor can the non-Jew be pronounced acquitted by unconsciously realizing its standard.

It is only by faith that one can be pronounced acquitted. God in his justness exhibited Jesus as a reconciling sacrifice; God pronounces men acquitted who believe. Acquittal is for everyone who believes, Jew or non-Jew. There are no exceptions; Abraham, for example, was pronounced acquitted not by the rite of circumcision, but because he believed. Nor may the descendents of Abraham think that their racial possession of the Law secures acquittal for them;

if it might, faith would be nullified. It is, rather, those descendents of Abraham in belief who have the status. Thus the promise of Scripture is realized: Abraham is the forefather of multitudes.

The candid and logical person will be aware of much in Paul's reasoning which is specious. There are several points which rest upon doubtful postulates, and others which do not come from their postulates. But the next statements are of even more questionable logic. For Paul goes on to infer that the status of the sinful person, i.e., of all except those pronounced acquitted, is the hereditary result of the guilt of the first man. Death reigned from Adam to Moses. Then the Law came, and, instead of enabling people to achieve the status of acquittal, offense was increased. The situation was utterly desperate until Jesus came, a new Adam. He effected what apart from him was impossible; only when one exercises faith in Jesus is one pronounced acquitted.

Now Paul becomes highly mystical, presenting elements in his teaching which are closely similar to elements in the mystery cults. The believer identifies himself with Christ; he is baptized into union with Christ, so that figuratively he experiences death as Christ did, and as Christ was raised from among the dead so the believer is raised to live a new spirit life.

The new spirit life is expected to be utterly different from the old flesh life. The believer used to sin grossly. Then, consciously or unconsciously, he was responsible to Law, which (as Paul has — to his satisfaction — " proved ") could not secure his acquittal. But one is released from amenability to Law when he dies; so the believer, having died with

Christ, is released from responsibility to Law — he is now a spirit-person.

Paul next protects himself from the implications that the discharge from legal amenability sanctions sinful living, or that the Law is an instrument of sin. In doing so he reveals his conceptions of the nature of men. He begins by using himself as an example; he was once alive and without amenability to Law, and therefore in sin. When he accepted amenability, Law, in teaching what was sinful, invested it with such attractiveness that desire to do what was sinful was stimulated, and the desire became so powerful that it could not be resisted. For there are different levels of the nature of men: the physical (literally, the flesh level) and the spiritual. One may know what he ought to do, and may wish to do it, and yet be unable to do it because the physical self dominates as long as one is a flesh-person. It is only when one is a spirit-person that he is able to live justly, and it is only when he is pronounced acquitted that he is a spirit-person. The faith of Christ is necessary to secure acquittal for him. Thus the round of Paul's reasoning is complete: God is just, man is evil, man can be pronounced acquitted only when he exercises faith in Christ who did what no man can do; therefore what Christ did in relation to the justness of God secures the pronouncement of acquittal for the man who believes.

This leads to a flight of high eloquence as Paul contemplates this perfect sequence. He draws a thoroughgoing distinction between the flesh and the spirit levels. He suggests effectively the status of the believer as a just person (i.e., as one who is pronounced acquitted). He movingly affirms that the Spirit (i.e., God's Spirit, the Holy Spirit) helps one and brings him to the consciousness that he is God's child. Further, there are implications which are nothing less than cosmic: all this was foreknown to God, who so ordered events that all creation has been in the agony of birth-pangs until the imminent *dénouement,* when even our bodies will be redeemed. God long ago predestined it; now he is bringing it to pass. He did not withhold his own Son, but freely offered him as a gift. Nothing can separate the believer from God's love. That is the joy of the acquitted.

Why did Paul present this involved and minutely reasoned argument? If he wished to impart some charismatic gift to his readers, what did he think that he was accomplishing by these teachings? Did his readers need to be taught that the Jew deserved a recognition which they had failed to accord him? It should never be forgotten that whatever was the result of Paul's leadership, or whatever his Jewish contemporaries thought of him, Paul has a manifest Jewish bias.

Again, was there current in the circle here addressed a view of the meaning of what Jesus had been and had done which Paul regarded as erroneous or inadequate? Were they too legalistic in their conception of the religious life? Had they used Jewish Scripture in such ways as to derive from them interpretations which Paul found it necessary to correct? [20] Was he fearful lest they should be exposed to teachings which he considered dangerous? Did he write to forestall error? These possibilities are clews to the religious problems basic to the writing of the document.

The second problem, discussed in Romans 9–11, may be stated simply. Paul reveals his intense disappointment that the Jewish people have rejected the good news of Jesus.

This presents a difficult problem. For in repudiating the normativity of Torah Paul never doubts the validity of Jewish Scripture on its non-statutory side. In these aspects of Scripture God made promises. These are necessarily valid. There are promises of a certain status for the Jewish people. But they have rejected Jesus, who was also promised in Scripture. It was intolerable to Paul that Scripture could be self-contradictory. What then? Does their rejection by Jesus mean that God has canceled his promise to the Jews? This, too, is intolerable. The promises are valid, despite appearances. Can the dilemma be solved?

Paul has a simple solution. It is that God has caused the Jewish people to refuse to believe. This is an arbitrary view of God, but Paul is able to adduce Scriptural examples of similarly arbitrary behavior of God. But, he goes on, this act was with reference to God's whole purpose; the Jewish rejection of Jesus caused the messengers to speak to the non-Jews. This was what God intended. The rejection will be temporary, for now that his hardening of Israel's heart has resulted in the evangelization of non-Jews, God will soon cause the Jews to believe.

This discussion, like others, is particularly valuable for its by-products. It tells much of Paul's religion. It shows how he used Scripture. Its evidence for understanding the relations between Jews and non-Jews in emerging Christianity is invaluable. It shows that when Paul wrote (about the year 58) nascent Christianity was thoroughly gentile. The failure of the preaching to the Jews was complete. It has been pointed out that there was much in the primitive preaching which unfitted it for Jewish reception. Paul's statements show that this was so. The Jewish people, with slight exception, had failed to accept it. Response had come from non-Jews. The transition to gentile publics was effected before Paul wrote these words, and its result was already apparent.

The remaining parts of Romans discuss several practical matters. Chapter 12 is directed to the encouragement of its readers to give freer rein to charismatic endowments. The chapter, although with opposite aim, assumes a place beside 1 Corinthians 12–14 as a revealing discussion of spirit gifts.

In the latter part of the same chapter advice of a paraenetic nature is given. Here the language resembles that of the gospels, so that it is sometimes thought that Paul here cites "teaching of Jesus," or quotes from the "oral tradition." This, however, is to mistake the matter entirely; the Paul who trusts in charismatic inspiration has no need to cite "teaching of Jesus," much less to quote a source. The proper perspective is reached when one remembers that "teaching of Jesus" has no place in what Paul wrote, and therefore presumably in what he preached and taught. "Teachings of Jesus" were merely in process of formulation during the years of Paul's activity; it is questionable that he knew any of these traditions, and improbable that he knew any considerable amount. It was different, of course, in the work of the non-Pauline leaders. The gospel traditions had their beginnings in this period; it does not follow that non-Pauline leaders were as unsympathetic to this trend as Paul was. But the discussion of this belongs to later sections of the present study.

Paul advises his readers concerning the right attitude toward civil government. His teaching is in complete agreement with traditional Pharisaic Judaism; civil government exists because God wills it; it is therefore necessary to be obedient to it and to discharge the duties thus entailed, including tax-payment and maintenance of respectful bearing toward officials; one ought not to resist government; one should be a scrupulously law-abiding subject. Characteristically, a contiguous paragraph stresses the imminence of the apocalyptic *dénouement* as sanction.

Then comes a discussion about dietary practices and the observance of special days. The advice is the same as that given the Corinthians: these matters are immaterial except as they affect other persons; in such case one should avoid giving offense.

But Paul here makes a remark which is extraordinarily revealing for what it implies. In writing about dietary customs he says: " I know; I have been persuaded by the Lord Jesus that nothing is common as such " (14:14). This statement, in connection with what follows, strongly suggests that Paul was anything but consistent in following Jewish dietary customs; no Jew who took Jewish teaching and practice as normative could say what Paul here says. It is clear that Paul in this situation, with a now long experience of the religion which he lived, did not observe Jewish customs and practices with any degree of strictness.

The remark is instructive otherwise, too. It is in characteristic Greek idiom: " I have been persuaded by the Lord Jesus," or, literally, " in the Lord Jesus." Now, this idiom [21] is familiar in Paul's writings. It is part of his mystical terminology.[22] It has important bearing with reference to Paul's religion; it indicates how Jesus was a source of his knowledge. How was he? In this connection, again, it is sometimes thought that Paul is citing a teaching of Jesus, of which Mark 7:1–23 is the literary witness, Mark 7:19 being cited here. But this is impossible; Mark 7:19 is not a saying of Jesus, but an editorial comment. In any case it would be out of keeping with the very nature of Paul's religion to cite some incident from the life of Jesus, or to quote, even from oral tradition; impossible for him to have quoted a gospel, since none was yet written.

It is much more probable that Paul had learned from ecstatic experience that no food was common as such; that it had been revealed to him in ecstasy that he and other believers might eat what was available. This is quite in line with what has otherwise and elsewhere been observed. It is in keeping with Paul's non-use of Jesus' teaching. It is evidence that experience of a definite type was basic in Pauline Christianity. It enables the investigator to see that customs and conventional behavior in Paul's groups were developed from experience, and that teachings about them were generalized from experience. To say then that they came from the Lord Jesus invested the teachings with powerful sanction.

The final items are partly hortatory, partly personal. In a restrained tone Paul expresses confidence in his readers. He tells them several things about his work. He says that it is by God's favor that he was made a minister of Christ among the non-Jews. He has had a measure of success, which has been exhibited by spoken words and by deeds, proved by omens, marvelous acts and spirit power. These remarks, too, illustrate the spiritistic nature of his religion. Now, having preached from Jerusalem to the environs of Illyricum, there is no further territory in this area to evangelize. It is noteworthy that Paul thought only of the parts of the east and the north Mediterranean, with no reference to Alexandria or Africa. He thought of going to Spain, stopping the while in Rome. But now he is going to take the collection gathered by the people of Macedonia and Greece to the people of Jerusalem; after this is done he hopes to go to Spain. In the meantime he is under serious apprehension of what may occur to him in Jerusalem; he asks his readers to " agonize " with him in prayer that he may escape from those in Judea who are disobedient, that the gift may be well received, and that he may then come to Rome. These revealing items throw into high light the differences between Pauline and non-Pauline Christianity. Although the details cannot be inferred, the expectation of possible violence is obvious, and the fact is significant.

The only consensus concerning the remaining letters attributed to Paul, i.e., Philippians, Colossians, Philemon and Ephesians, is the custom of regarding them together and calling them " prison epistles." However, the traditional theory (based upon the last chapter of Luke-Acts) that they were written from Rome, has been challenged by the attractive theory that certain of them were written while Paul was imprisoned in Ephesus [23] (or as a recent study of three of them infers, Caesarea).[24] There is serious doubt, of course, of Paul's authorship of Colossians and Ephesians.[25]

It is advisable to hold in abeyance any judgment of the place of writing of the " prison epistles." This is not because dating thus becomes a difficult problem. It is now known, for example, that the quasi-Gnosticism combatted in Colossians may well have been in existence at the time involved by the theory of an Ephesian imprisonment.[26] As for the alleged high doctrine about Jesus, it is difficult to see anything in Philippians or Colossians which is " higher " than the conception of Jesus which is found in unquestioned Pauline letters. In these Jesus is a person of divine status or nature whose reconciling work was nothing short of cosmic in its effect. There is nothing in the three " prison epistles " which might not have been written by Paul in the time required by the new theory.

The problems of Ephesians are more difficult. Until recently there has been current, aside from the traditional view of Pauline authorship, only one view of the writing of Ephesians which rests upon an adequate analysis of evidence. No one has studied the work with more patience, industry or careful reasoning than that evinced by H. J. Holtzmann, whose research represents the first thoroughgoing analysis of Ephesians and an investigation of its relations with Colossians.[27] The second critical view is that of Professor E. J. Goodspeed, whose study [28] deserves as close attention as that of Holtzmann. It does not offer merely a rationale for the negative judgment of authorship, but accounts for the writing of the pseudonymous letter by discovering its intended purpose. This was the acute perception, by a church leader during the days of Domitian, that Paul's letters are particularly instructive when they are read together, and that when they are read together they teach not merely the churches to which they were written, but all the churches — indeed, the " Church." Consequently this unidentified leader collected such of Paul's letters as were available, and " published " them, i.e., caused them to be copied and circulated together. Following certain literary models, he wrote what is now called the Letter to the Ephesians as an introductory covering letter. Originally the pseudonymous letter had no place name; that " in Ephesus " is an intrusion into the text is well known; how the words got there cannot be determined.

Since Professor Goodspeed's study of Ephesians and some of its implications seem to be convincing, discussion of Ephesians will be omitted from the present section. It will occur in its proper place, as an aspect of the Christianity of the gospel-making period.

To resume the proper theme, the discussion of Philippians should be made first, if for no other reason than Lightfoot's incisive observations.[29] In it the atmosphere of imprisonment is plain. The people of Philippi, hearing that Paul was a prisoner, sent assistance to him by Epaphroditus. Unfortunately the messenger fell ill, and Paul had to care for him. Now that he is able, Paul is sending him home. He urges the Philippians to receive him. There are other references to imprisonment (1:7, 14; 2:23).

However, the atmosphere of Philippians does not seem to be the same throughout the " letter." This should be kept in mind when it is observed that " seams " appear clearly in several places. Together, and in conjunction with still other evidence, these data strongly suggest the composite nature of Philippians. Professor Goodspeed's translation of 3:1 is doubtless correct: " Now, my brothers, good-bye." This is the usual sense of the Greek word $\chi\alpha\acute{\iota}\rho\epsilon\tau\epsilon$. Thus 3:2 must be a different letter. Compare also 4:4. The abruptness with which Philippians proceeds requires the judgment that several letters have been edited together. A reference in a later writing corroborates this. Polycarp of Smyrna, in a letter to Philippi, remarks that Paul wrote " letters " to them (Epistle of Polycarp, 3:2). While this might apply to our Philippians and to lost letters, it is likely that it alludes to composite parts edited together to make our letter.

The content of the "letter" presents some difficult problems. Lohmeyer suggests that 2:5–10 is a pre-Pauline hymn.[30] He also stresses the data of persecution in the source, finding in them the underlying theme. He develops these hypotheses attractively, but it can hardly be said that he demonstrates his points.

Another difficulty is in the anti-Jewish passage of 3:2ff, the bitterest and most venomous anti-Jewish polemic found in Paul's writings. It is extremely odd that Paul should have referred to circumcision in the sarcastic epithet, "cutting." It was not usual for Paul to ridicule Jewish custom! Why was he impelled to affirm his own Jewishness so strongly in 3:4ff? If the situation in Philippi was as sketched in Luke-Acts (Acts 16:11–40) it is the more strange, for Luke-Acts implies that there were not enough Jews there to form a synagogue. Had Jewish opposition developed later? Or is this a fragment of a Pauline letter originally written with reference to another situation? However it may be, the data are valuable for what they disclose about Paul's early life and subsequent religious attitudes.

Non-Pauline leaders are plainly referred to in Philippians 1:15–18. The non-Pauline elements in the emerging Christian movement have been mentioned. Here is explicit reference to their activity.

The letter to the Colossians, as is well known, is often regarded as un-Pauline. Yet it is not mere conservatism to point out the flaws in the logic which is usually followed. Hardly a single modern rejection of Colossians adds anything to the judgment expressed nearly a century ago by Baur.

This is because until recently it was believed that every form of Gnosticism was a late adaptation to Hellenism, so that a document tinged by it could not have been written by Paul. It is now known that Gnosticism was part of the whole trend by which Oriental influence in religion and thought became influential in the West; it is also known that the syncretism began early. In the light of these data Lohmeyer investigated Colossians anew. The result of his work [31] shows that there is nothing in the data of the syncretistic religions which precludes the writing of the letter in Paul's lifetime or by Paul himself.

The content of the letter about the nature or the status of Jesus needs to be viewed similarly. For Paul Jesus was always a divine figure, whose work was cosmic in scope. The high doctrine about Jesus does not determine that the letter is un-Pauline.

Colossians does, however, differ from indisputably Pauline letters in the degree to which it uses language and conceptions of Hellenistic religions, particularly the mystery cults. The difference is not so great between Colossians and certain parts of the Corinthian correspondence, and there are striking parallels elsewhere (e.g., Romans 6:2ff). On the whole, the influence of the mystery cults upon Paul, while it is denied by many, is obvious.[32] A difference which, as in this case, is one of degree, is not of much importance.

More significant is the liturgical quality of the language of Colossians. A careful examination of the style of Paul's letters bears out the observation that this is a unique feature. It must be taken into account in studying the question of authorship.

Perhaps the most important question concerns the nature

of the teaching in Colossians 3:18–4:1. These homely advices stood there long before their nature was observed. The approach from the standpoint of form led to this discovery. Weidinger[33] recognized the passage as an example of the "table of household duties" which generalized particular items of ethic common in the Hellenistic world. He carefully studied the passage in the light of its parallels in the Graeco-Roman and the alleged Hellenistic-Jewish literatures. He showed that in this and other examples found in early Christian writings the current Christian leader merely took over in his *Haustafel* the conventional moral pattern which existed in his time and place. Such "Christianization" as was given was but slight and elementary; in the present case if the words "in the Lord" or "fearing the Lord" are omitted, the code does not differ from conventional Stoic morality.

Not that it constitutes a problem to discover that part of a Pauline letter was derived from contemporary sources. This passage constitutes a problem because it raises a fundamental question about the very nature of the religion promoted by it. It has been shown that Paul does not cite authorities and use sources in his ethical teaching. When he does derive something "from the Lord" he gets it by ecstasy. Here, if Weidinger is right, a code is used with but slight adaptation. What does this imply?

A thorough study of Paul's ethical teaching emphasizes the problem. Why should Paul, to whom the end of the age was imminent, have taught ethical codes? Why should so highly spiritistic a teacher have taught here as though life was not spiritistic? Answers to these questions have been too simple. It is usually thought that Paul derived his ethic from Judaism; that Pauline Christianity is merely the joining of gentile cult conceptions and Jewish ethics. Some have thought that Stoicism was the source of Paul's ethic. But such judgments do not penetrate to the ultimate problem: since Paul conceived the religious life as he did, why did he promulgate an objective ethical code?

Weidinger throws the problem into high relief. The implication of his discussion constitutes the most serious difficulty in maintaining the Pauline authorship of Colossians. For there is no example of the *Haustafeln* in any other Pauline letter. Moral exhortation (or paraenesis) there is. But the ethical teaching of other letters is almost always specific and with reference to the particular situation of the given letter. Generalized code or pattern is found only here. In this Colossians is unique.

It has been suggested that the date of Colossians gives a clew; that in his later days Paul had changed in a number of fundamental respects, so that he was not then averse to making use of such values. Indeed, all the " prison epistles " are sometimes considered as the " later " as distinct from the " earlier epistles." [34] For example, it has been suggested that Paul's thought about the end of the age underwent " development." [35] But evidence for this and for other instances is scant. It is doubtful that a few years in Paul's life had such profound effect. His literary activity was brief; " development " during the period is improbable, and certainly it would not have been caused merely by the passing of time. Paul's pre-literary period was longer; if development occurred it would have been during these formative years. When he began to write his mind was made up; it is unlikely that it changed in any important respect or degree.

It must be concluded that the presence of a *Haustafel* in a Pauline letter is abnormal. Does it follow that the letter is ungenuine?

To be sure, a certain strangeness in Colossians is natural. As in the case of Romans, Paul's lack of personal acquaintance with the readers may account for the less familiar tone in the letter.

Other striking elements in Colossians include the assertion of highly honorific qualities to the nature of Christ, and the combatting of popular ascetic tendencies. The language approaches the terminology of the mystery cults much more obviously than is usual in a Pauline letter. The emphasis upon the mystical relation of the believer with Christ is very strong. The letter expects the believer to become a spirit-person. The point is explicit: the ideal is that he become one with Christ, and therefore a pneumatic; his physical nature then is dead; he has put aside all the behavior which characterized him as a flesh-person. He is then a new self. It matters not whether he had been Greek or Jew, non-Greek or a savage, slave or freeman — what matters is that Christ is all and in all.

It is then to be expected that behavior in the spirit life will be in proper character with it. The spirit life has its virtues, which Colossians cites, going on to point out the usefulness of sharing in the religious assembly. At this point the *Haustafel* occurs, with directions to married women and men, children, fathers and slaves.

With reference to the situation in the Colossian church, Lohmeyer's study has made it easier to believe that some form of Gnosticism existed in Paul's churches during his lifetime. Every element of mystical and ascetic religion to be observed in the Colossian situation (e.g., the worship of heavenly bodies, keeping special days and ascetic practices) is to be found in the Asian and Phrygian territories between which Colossae was located. The crossing of these tendencies with Judaism is also to be observed there, with the addition of circumcision and dietary customs. Paul obviates the special validity of these by subsuming every possible religious value under Christ as the divine fulness (or *pleroma,* using a term common in the Gnostic systems). These have the status accorded the Law in the other letters: they were natural elements in the religious life of people who have not learned about Christ. Indeed, the people were enslaved to them until Christ came. Now, however, one may respond to the preaching of Christ, who then becomes the head of all. The believer becomes in union with him, and all the former elements of his religious life are invalidated. The believer then owes it to Christ, with whom he is in union, not to continue in his former ways. He is a new creature, and he should live accordingly. The observance of special days, dietary distinctions, angel-worship, ascetic abstinence, self-humiliation, enslavement to the " elements of the cosmos " — these are all secondary to the mystical relation with Christ, which renders them all unnecessary. It is idle to regard these teachings as mere anti-Jewish or anti-Gnostic polemic; they indicate an advanced adaptation to elements in Paul's total religious background.

The personal references in Colossians are of value. The letter is closely related to " Philemon," and the reference to the letter to the Laodiceans presents a problem which will be discussed presently. The note that (Aristarchus?) Mark and Jesus-Justus are the only converts from Judaism who have been of any comfort to Paul ought to be taken in the light of Romans 9–11; it is another proof that the response of Jews to the primitive preaching was so slight that thus early the number of Jewish leaders was negligible.

The little letter " to Philemon " closely resembles the many non-literary papyri of the Hellenistic period. But its contents are by no means of inconsiderable importance. Indeed, if Professor Goodspeed's view, followed here, attains general acceptance the common attitude toward the letter will be revolutionized. As he shows, it is not to Philemon alone. It is addressed to Philemon, Apphia, Archippus, *and to the church which meets in Philemon's house*. It is not a letter to an individual, but another letter to a church.

The letter was written because at some time while Paul was in prison (probably in Ephesus, not far from Laodicea and Colossae) he had " converted " a runaway slave, one Onesimus,[36] the property of Philemon (or Archippus?). Paul sent him back to his owner, and sent (presumably with him) this letter.

Its message is simple: those addressed are exhorted to receive and welcome Onesimus; it is hoped that he will be treated not as a runaway slave but as a brother in Christ. It is delicately suggested that he be sent back as a freedman to be Paul's helper. Paul subtly points out that it is owed him to have these things done. The expectation is strengthened as the church is addressed together with the responsible individuals.

The importance of the message appears when it is recalled that the usual treatment of a recaptured slave was severe in the extreme. His owner had the power of life and death over him; if he should cause him to be beaten so severely that he died the owner was not culpable. Presumably some punishment would have been meted out to Onesimus if he had been returned without the benefit of Paul's letter. It was, surely, a serious matter for Paul to send him back.

It will be remembered that Paul urged the Colossians to send his letter to them to the group at Laodicea, and to have the letter to the latter sent to Colossae. If Professor Goodspeed's theory is correct, this would place the force of the Colossian church, too, behind the request made in "Philemon," thus bringing further sanction to bear. The hypothesis, otherwise attractive, is also forceful in this aspect.

What of the final days of Paul's life? This study has made no attempt to state, even briefly, the available facts of Paul's "life." It has had as its objective merely to summarize the characteristics of Paul as a religious leader, to observe what may be learned of his religious life and leadership, and to view him in relation to the emerging and growing Christian movement. It has repeatedly emphasized the presence of pre-Pauline and of non-Pauline Christianity. It has cautioned against regarding "Pauline Christianity" as normative or as typical of all Christianity. It has sought to be free from the error of supposing that when one has read a "life" of Jesus and of Paul he has thereby been informed of the genesis and growth of Christianity.

Yet the probable historical events of Paul's last days are instructive of situations in the evolution of Christianity. The "prison letters" represent more than one experience and more than one time of writing. Doubtless the fears of what might happen in Jerusalem were realized; when Paul went to Jerusalem he went to an untoward fate which resulted in his death. Whatever critical reconstruction of the later chapters of Luke-Acts is required, whatever result of the necessary criticism of extra-biblical tradition is reached, it is probable that Paul met his death by execution at the hands of the State.

Paul came to be particularly revered when he was invested by tradition with the martyr's role. This, more than his life-work, made secure his status in Christian esteem. Yet it was to be credited to him that when he met his death he had evangelized much of the territory of the north Mediterranean, and had planted there a number of important churches. That these were in most cases at strategically important points [37] may or may not have been intended by Paul; they were in fact strategically located, and they were well enough founded that they endured. That he wrote letters while executing his task was incidental to his purposes, but the fortunate accidents of their writing and preservation brings to modern study a relatively considerable bulk of important source material.

The presence beside Paul's communities of groups of early " Christians " whose religious lives differed in characteristic ways from Paul's conceptions in no wise detracts from Paul's achievements. It is necessary to study these indications of non-Pauline Christianity, however, as it is necessary to study the religious lives of the people of Paul's churches and of Paul himself. Such study enables the student to discover significant developments in these non-Pauline circles, and to observe their contributions to the growth of Christianity.

V

NON–PAULINE CHRISTIANITY BEFORE
THE GOSPELS

THE GOSPEL MATERIALS

A number of generalizations about the early growth of
" Christianity " have been made. The movement began
when certain persons spoke of having " seen " Jesus after his
death. They told their stories to anyone and all who would
listen. Soon there grew up several small groups of people
who believed them. These groups were early to be found in
several places in and outside the land of Israel. They early
became inclusive of Jews and of non-Jews, and it was not
long until the non-Jews outnumbered the Jews.

Such was the situation when Paul, about whom more is
known than about any other early leader, came upon the
scene. He spread the growing cults of Jesus in many localities of the north shore of the Mediterranean. His influence
resulted in the currency in these communities of a particular
type of religious experience.

But before Paul and during his activity non-Pauline trends
were present in emerging Christianity. These must not be
overlooked.

It was emphasized that in the Pauline letters, and thus
probably also in the Pauline preaching, there is little reference to Jesus' career. Aside from a few passing remarks, from

which an occasional datum may be inferred, there is very little to be learned about Jesus, and still less about his teaching, from Paul.

Why was it so? One reason was suggested: Paul's conception of religion was one to which these features were not germane. Charismatic inspiration was normal in Paul's religion. Literary or oral sources of knowledge, even of Jesus' life and teaching, were gratuitous. Jewish Scripture was indeed used, but this the more accentuates the fact that Jesus' life and teaching were not.

True, Paul's preaching resembled that of other early messengers in giving central place to Jesus' death and resurrection. About these themes there was an early and a constantly growing tradition, which Paul, like every other preacher, used in some form. This does not, however, contradict the fact that in the writings, and presumably in the preaching, of Paul there is the barest minimum of reference to the life and teaching of Jesus. It may therefore be concluded that if other leaders had been like Paul, or if Christianity generally had been like the religion of the Pauline communities, the gospels as we have them would never have developed. It follows, then, that the growth of the gospels furnishes a number of clews for the study of non-Pauline Christianity.

The growth of the gospels has long interested scholars. In general, when it became customary to study the gospels individually (that is, not harmonistically) and comparatively, two theories of their origin arose. Obviously the first three are more or less similar to one another, and these three differ from the fourth. A study of the first three discovered a number of detailed similarities (some involving all three, others involving two of the three) and certain individual differences. Items were observed in which two of the three agreed together against a third. These phenomena suggest that the gospels are related to one another. An early generalization was that Mark, similar to but briefer than Matthew and Luke, was an abridged epitome of these. But when thorough analysis was made this idea was reversed: it was shown that Mark was prior to and a source of the others.[1]

Another theory was that the relations of the gospels were not literary at all, but that the stories of Jesus, originally told orally, attained fixed form, so that the four gospels represent the writing of as many forms of oral tradition.[2] This theory enjoyed wide currency for a time. It offers a simple explanation of the *differences* between the gospels.

But theories of literary relationship inevitably superseded the oral hypothesis, for the *similarities* in the gospels cannot be explained by it. Presently appeared the theory which until recently held all but universal sway: that the sources of the first three gospels are two: Mark and another source which was found in some total of the materials similar in Matthew and Luke but not paralleled in Mark.[3] This hypothetical source was referred to by the symbol "Q" (for *Quelle,* source), and the hypothesis was called the Two Source, or the Two Document Hypothesis.

A little reflection shows that this simple explanation of the relations of the first three gospels does not account for all the facts. It leaves out of consideration the materials in a gospel which are not paralleled in another. Some of the materials are only roughly similar in two or three (or the four) gospels; close inspection makes it doubtful that two (or more) accounts of the same item are before one's eye. Often items similar in language are in widely different positions in the gospels. These considerations make it very difficult to determine the content of the "second source"; when scholars offered "reconstructions" of "Q" their differences caused the hypothesis to break down.

Consequently there appeared a theory that the sources of the synoptic gospels number more than two. Thirty years ago a study of the first three gospels [4] suggested that a multiple source hypothesis, rather than a two source theory, was required by the facts. According to this study, the accounts of Jesus' birth and infancy represent two sources, Mark was another. Since Luke has much in his Passion Story which is without parallel, a special source here was identified. The materials of Matthew for which there was no parallel elsewhere indicate a source. Then, finally, the materials paralleled in Matthew and Luke, but not found in Mark, were found to contain two sources, and it was suggested that one of these was probably composite.

Twenty years later two theories, advanced at the same time, but arrived at independently, were published.[5] These suggested that the sources of the first three gospels numbered four: Mark, a document represented by the peculiar materials of Matthew, a source named by the old symbol "Q" (although it was defined as of different content), and another made up of some of the materials of the old "Q" but called "L." Both theories developed new judgments about the use of Mark as a source in Matthew and Luke, and a new theory about the origin of Luke. Older theories regarded Mark as the primary source of Matthew and Luke, into which the non-Marcan materials were introduced. The new theories are that while Matthew proceeded in this way, the first form of Luke consisted of the materials of Q plus

L; this "Proto-Luke" was the first draft from which the present Luke was made by incorporating the Marcan materials into it.[6]

These interesting features obtained for this form of the multiple source theory a wide currency, a distinction never accorded the early form. However, a critical perspective shows clearly that the later formulations of the theory are hardly more than a conservative or even a half-way step in the direction much more logically developed in the earlier essay.

The most recent research directs attention to still more minute detail. The multiple source hypothesis, even in the form which identifies the largest number of sources,[7] still deals with fairly extensive aggregations of gospel materials. What may be said of the materials themselves?

The gospels contain a number of brief stories about Jesus and a number of his sayings. Sometimes the stories are purely narrative, stories of something which he did, a "miracle," a journey, or an exploit. Sometimes the stories contain sayings; there are also sententious sayings and dialogue. There are narrative sayings, e.g., parables. Some sayings are of such miscellaneous nature that their place beside one another seems to have been purely arbitrarily assigned by the evangelist.

A number of scholars analyzed the gospel materials anew. One compared the gospels with other writings of their period,[8] discovering their place in general literary development. They were found to be non-literary, or unliterary, in character. They do not attempt elegance of writing. They are practical. Their contents relate to the purposes of the advancement of the religious movement from which they came. Another study analyzed the "framework" of the story of Jesus.[9] It showed that the gospels consist of a number of individual parts, or sections (the technical term is "pericopes") which have been brought together by the gospel writers in quite arbitrary fashion, the individual pericopes bound together by typical and conventional formulae. It is a startling fact that nothing in the pericopes binds them together by nature; when the "binders" are removed the individual sections fall apart.

Two studies analyzed the separate pericopes.[10] These were found to be classifiable. They are, in fact, several examples of a few types of narratives or sayings. They were identified by their literary form, so that studies of them came to be called *Formgeschichte* (inadequately translated as "form-history," or "form-criticism"[11]). What may be learned of the origin of these pericopes?

The earliest and most constant element in the stories about Jesus was the theme of his death and resurrection. The Passion Story is the oldest and the most constantly renewed theme in the story of Jesus. This was the story which the earliest evangelists told. For some it was, indeed, the story of their experience. Those who heard them and believed repeated their stories. If the bare and simple stories grew in number, volume, and adornment in detail this is only what might be expected; the differences between the several extant narratives are less than they might readily have been.

The growth of stories of Jesus' death and resurrection naturally required some reflection about Jesus' nature. He who had so remarkable a fate must have been a remarkable person. Who was he? Not that there was detail about Jesus' birth, lineage or career in any primitive stage. The probabilities are that the earliest speculations about Jesus' nature were those which led, on the one hand, to his identification as God's Anointed, and, on the other hand, to the telling of stories about his remarkable deeds as a spirit-filled person. It is an irresistible guess that Jesus was thus early identified as the One who was to come on the clouds as an apocalyptic Anointed. This is about the stage of reflection which one sees in the religion of Paul. Paul insists that God revealed his Son in him, from which revelation he learned such things as that Jesus had died for our sins, had been raised from among the dead, had appeared to certain persons, is now in heaven whence he shall come to raise all from the dead and to bring in the Reign of God. Certainly others engaged in such reflection and made comparable identifications.

Another line of development was easy and natural. There were many cults in the Graeco-Roman world in which dying and rising savior-gods were central figures. When the stories of Jesus' death and resurrection were told in such circles it was inevitable that they should take forms typical in these cults. The hero-cults likewise furnished a type of cult narrative toward which the story of Jesus was attracted.

Ceremonial was an influence in this connection, since it was an early development in the emergence of Christianity. The sacramental character of the eucharistic meal obtained early; in this ceremony the dramatic representation of Jesus' death was central. The cult meal was a pole about which stories of Jesus early began and long continued to cohere.

Even relatively late New Testament sources show many different interests in their references to Jesus' death. They attempt to fix the responsibility for it: Luke-Acts tells that Peter and Paul with more than one strong thrust of polemic repeatedly attach the blame upon the Jewish people. It is not likely that the speeches carrying this theme have any likelihood of historicity, but they illustrate the fact that the story of Jesus' death was told with polemical interpretation.

Polemic is also found in many of the gospel pericopes. The story of Jesus and his followers walking through the grainfields, the while preparing grain for food, with objection from opponents and defense by Jesus, is an example. This story has as its central element the saying about the sabbath being made for man, not man for the sabbath. Dibelius and Bultmann both regard it as primitive, a pericope which arose in a Palestinian community. There are several other polemical stories.[12] This interest found its way into the gospel materials very early.

While it is a far call from the earliest pericopes to the final forms of the gospels, at relatively early times stories of Jesus came into use in the propagation of the Christian movement. They grew into the traditions because they were useful. Dibelius believes that the primitive stories were used in the early mission preaching.[18] It cannot be doubted that the competition which advocates of the new movement met in their enthusiastic efforts would make relevant just such stories as the gospel materials contain.

For example, competition would be furnished by the mystery cults, each of which had its cult legend of the death and the triumph over death of its cult Lord. Again, a popular competitor was the healing cult of the hero-god Aesklepius. What would be more natural than for the stories of Jesus as a healer to be reported in response to similar stories told of Aesklepius? In such a way competition accounts for much of the content of the gospel materials.

Another element, less primitive than these motives, must be observed. It appears as one notices the difference between Pauline and non-Pauline Christianity. It is the rise and growth of teaching of Jesus. It has already been pointed out that this interest was developed in non-Pauline Christianity. For the gospel materials witness the fact that not all early Christians found charismatic inspiration congenial or sufficient. The didactic materials of the gospels arose as certain sections of early Christianity found themselves faced with the necessity of discovering new patterns, norms and sanctions for the guidance of cult members. To be sure, questions about the moral life presumably arose in the cults secondarily to the early stages of evangelization. But ethical questions emerged soon. The Pauline letters prove this; hardly had a community been evangelized and a house-church founded when moral problems arose.

It must be remembered that in the early stages of the movement the cults of Jesus were not consciously " Christian." Their particular character was something yet to be achieved. Either the cult members would be characterized by their common habits and customs, or some otherwise developed standard must be imposed. Doubtless for leaders who were Jewish it would be natural to urge the code which was familiar in the circle in which they had been brought up. Or, if they were not Jewish, leaders might inculcate such other code as that to which they were accustomed. In whatever case it was necessary and inevitable, if the cults of Jesus were to achieve their own individuality, that they must develop their particular morality.

It is possible to observe certain of the steps by which their moral attitudes, which came to be regarded as " Christian," grew up. The materials of the gospels represent stages in this process. For the gospels may be viewed as articulations of ways of life which were crystallized into norms and patterns by the experiences of the cult members in their group relationships. That they were ascribed to Jesus as his " teachings " (it should be remembered that the term implies a modern interest which was foreign to the gospel writers) was to secure sanction for them.

The gospel materials, when viewed in terms of their units, are of varying dates, or of varying levels of primitivity. There were several stages in their growth. By the time the gospels assumed their present forms a large mass of materials was available for their writers. The growth of these materials, however, goes back to the earliest stages of the emergence of Christianity. The gospel materials, considered as such, take the student to the pre-gospel stage of development, since, obviously, the gospel materials antedate the writing of the gospels as such.

The picture which the student should have in mind is that in the days before the gospels the advocates of the cults of Jesus had at their disposal a large repertoire of stories about the Lord of their cult, stories which from early times were of several types. These were used for purposes of evangelistic propaganda, for the advancement of the cults, for effecting their expansion into new localities, for inducing new members to adhere to the cults, and for furnishing moral guidance in the lives of members as the cults assumed more definite corporate form. Undoubtedly the early preachers knew and used many stories and sayings which are not preserved in any of the streams of tradition known to subsequent Christianity; the popular tales of the " heretical " and the " apocryphal " gospels are examples. Much which was once in the tradition failed to be preserved.

It will also be kept in mind that in the early stages of the evolution of the gospel materials they were transmitted orally. It is a primary emphasis in the newer work on gospel origins that the materials assumed fixed form (as did folk tales) while they were spoken.

The materials were presently collected; or, rather, they began to cohere. Several items of stories or sayings of a given form, e.g., polemical stories, parables, miracle stories, grew into groups. From this it was but a step to their reduction to writing; there were gospel sources before there were gospels. This was a relatively late stage in the process, of course. However, at certain points in the evolution of the gospel materials they grew into sufficient volume and aggregated together so that their character as sources may be observed. In some cases varying levels of primitivity may be perceived, so that some may be recognized as earlier, some as later.

If the gospel materials and, later, the gospels, owe their production to non-Pauline Christianity, it is fortunate that there was sufficient difference among types of early Christian living to have caused the production of gospel materials, their growth into gospel sources, and, finally, the appearance of gospels. Basically it was the development of other than charismatic methods of dealing with moral living which caused the rise of gospels. Opposition of one cult legend to another, citation of Jesus as cult hero or redeeming god, identification of him as Anointed — such later impulses as these are next seen. These led to further growth of materials, to the evolution of sources, and to the production of gospels as such.

The ultimate materials of the gospels, as was shown, consist of the numerous stories and sayings which the gospels contain. Undoubtedly there were many such which did not find their way into the known gospels. The saying, " It is more blessed to give than to get," is an example; the sayings of the papyri, introduced by the simple formula, " Jesus says," are further instances; the pericope about the man working on sabbath in the Codex Bezae and the stories of the apocryphal gospels illustrate the wider currency of the materials.

The early Christian preaching was marvelously creative; it was prolific in the production of gospel materials, as is shown by the unique items in Luke-Acts and the Fourth Gospel. The processes which produced the gospel materials were operative from an early time. In their variety many different items of a number of forms came into use. Furthermore, the processes were continuous; the influences which were at work were steadily and fruitfully operative.

The first phase of the process, i.e., the production of the gospel materials, the pericopes of the present gospels and the many such materials of lost gospels or materials which did not find their way into gospels, was followed by a phase in which the materials began to be collected, or to cohere together. The crystallization of stories of Jesus' death and resurrection early led to the growth of passion stories.[14] The polemical stories similarly tended to adhere.[15] The fourth chapter of Mark is a collection [16] of parables with suitable narrative setting and conclusion; one may see how such a collection grew by comparing the group in Matthew 13. The interest in the end of the age caused an assembly of sayings in Mark 13; this was doubtless a source.[17] The process of growth may be seen, again, by comparing with this the forms which it assumed in Matthew 24 and Luke 21.

It is a common judgment that the later gospel writers knew and used Mark; that Mark is both a gospel and a gospel source. The differences between Mark and parallels to Mark in Matthew and Luke are instructive; if, indeed, it was Mark (as distinct from pericopes of which Mark was composed), the manner in which Mark was used gives much information of the use of gospel sources. When the consummate artist who produced the work which is feebly called Luke-Acts remarks in his conventional preface that by this time " many had taken in hand to draw up accounts " it is idle to speculate whether he had gospels or merely gospel sources in mind. To be sure, the data found when Luke-Acts is compared with Mark, Matthew and the Fourth Gospel point to the use of sources. Can one see how these grew?

It should be observed, as a prefatory remark, that too much has been made of the gospel sources in scholarly research. Or, to put it otherwise, wrong use has been made of the appearance of gospel sources as a phase of the evolution of gospels. It has been tacitly assumed that when sources have been identified, and when it has been shown that a gospel writer used these sources in the production of his work, the full story of his task has been told. It should be seen, on the other hand, that this carries the study of the processes only to an intermediate stage; it still remains to show how the sources were produced.

Another effort which has had but inadequate result is the effort to " reconstruct " gospel sources. While the probability may be established that the writer of Matthew used a " peculiar " sayings source, it is by no means certain that the source may be completely identified. It is highly probable that the writer of Luke-Acts used an individual source in his telling of the Passion Story, but it is highly conjectural to assert what its original form was.

Errors of detail in the criticism of gospel sources have been perpetrated. The judgment that an attempt to delineate the contents of the hypothetical " Q " resulted in " a heap of interesting ruins " may now be applied to the entire movement represented by the two document hypothesis.[18] It is pathetic that the several scholars who devoted many years of effort to " reconstruct " the non-Marcan source supposed that in placing this " document " beside Mark they had solved the synoptic problem. Undoubtedly it was a step in advance when it was shown that the sources of the gospels were several in number, rather than two. But again, it is regrettable that years after the original discovery was made a conservative theory of four sources, rather than the distinctive theory of multiple sources, was the one which found widespread acceptance.

Another source theory which is accorded more serious entertainment than it deserves is the abstraction that underlying the extant gospels were Aramaic (and Hebrew) gospels or gospel sources which were merely translated by our gospel writers.[19] Perhaps the major reason why this conjecture has been entertained is that Aramaic is not widely known by New Testament scholars, so that any considerable exhibit of Aramaic statistics is sufficiently impressive that competent scholars are sometimes disinclined to criticize it. However, the hypothesis is rejected by scholars of unquestionable critical acumen and ability.[20] When subjected to thorough test, its faulty logic [21] seriously undermines confidence, and it is shown to be only a curiously conservative abstraction which fails to meet the requirements set forth by the historical study of Christianity.

For what is desired in the study of the growth of gospels is knowledge of the processes by which Christianity itself grew. The ultimate units of the gospel traditions were produced by a variety of motives. Some had their source in the historical Jesus. These are definitely Jewish in character. Others were produced in the religious living of members and adherents of the cults of Jesus; of these some exhibit Jewish characteristics, while others are shown by their nature to have been produced in Hellenistic communities.

It is of fundamental importance that while certain of the gospel materials were produced in Palestine, and that while some of the tendencies toward the aggregation of these materials may be observed at this stage, *the gospel as such was the creation of the Hellenistic communities.*[22] This is in line with the recognition that important processes operated in the expansion of Christianity to occasion the transition from the *telling* of stories about Jesus to the *writing* of collected materials which were ascribed to him. These were highly important processes in Christianity's growth. One may interrogate the aggregated materials and thus discover the processes.

It has long been observed that Mark is the earliest gospel. It is plain that no source, either of Mark or of a later gospel, has the characteristics of a gospel. Gospel sources were materials of which, with others, the gospels were made. Unless Mark itself is an exception,[23] the sources lacked the essential nature of gospels.[24]

In " reconstructions " of " Q," of " Proto-Luke," and of the hypothetical documents of the Burton-Goodspeed theory some inspection of these materials may be made. What impression do these alleged documents make? The judgment may be offered that such work as has been done upon them indicates that the strongest case may be made for the peculiar sources of Matthew and Luke, i.e., the " Matthean " document of Burton-Goodspeed and Streeter, and the " Jerusalem " source of Burton-Goodspeed.[25]

The latter source illustrates the point that the Passion Story contains the oldest and newest elements of the story of Jesus; additions were constantly made to its materials. It is rewarding to inspect the materials characteristic of this formulation. These include elements which apparently arose in response to a number of interests of the people for whom they were included: political, cult, and other institutional interests.

Political interests, to note these first, are reflected in the particular references to the fall of Jerusalem and in the unique story of the review of Jesus' case by Herod Antipas, with the note that its issue was the renewal of friendship between Herod and Pilate. These items carry the lively interest in political matters which characterizes Luke-Acts throughout.

Cult interests in the so-called Jerusalem source are found in the important additions to and changes of the Marcan form of the story of the eucharistic meal. The Lucan story goes far toward the point reached by the Fourth Gospel, in which the event is not the Passover meal at all. In Luke-Acts it is treated as a proleptic observance of the Eucharist. It is striking that reference to Peter's denial is worked in, with its expression of the hope that the sorry tale may establish the fate of others;[26] the use of the Eucharist to strengthen the wavering in situations of persecution, so effective in later times,[27] is significant as appearing thus early.

The institutional interests of the source center chiefly in its rational explanation of Jesus' death. This is made in several ways. First, in the story itself much of the tone of the Fourth Gospel is present: Jesus is pictured as much less controlled by outward forces, much more as master of his situation. He always carries himself with dignity, even when he suffers indignity. The most distinctive feature is the explanation given by the resurrected Jesus himself; he makes all plain *by showing his followers how to understand Scripture*. This witnesses a line of activity which was in rapidly widening use: the pragmatic use of Scripture to explain things developed the institutional use of a whole body of literature.

A study of the peculiar " sayings source " of Matthew offers certain suggestions. First, the didactic nature of the materials implies, at least from the view of social history, that the needs of its readers or hearers were such as to call forth the document. Second, the materials include several types of teaching, the direct discourse (in which the evangelist's hand as editor may be seen), the parable, and miscellaneous sententious logia. The inference is that several forms were developed in different sections of growing Christianity.

The content of the materials is informing. Vital needs of the early Christians are observable. Anti-Jewish polemic is obvious, clearly showing that competition of cults of Jesus with Jewish communities largely accounts for the form and substance of many of the elements of the source. The polemic is both practical and theoretical; practical in that many of the elements of the crystallizing " Christian " ways of life were determined in conscious opposition to Jewish practices. For example, the members of the cults are expected to give alms, to pray and to fast, but differently from the ways in which members of synagogues did these things. Theoretical anti-Jewish polemic is found in the several parables, the theme of which is the displacement of Jews in favor of the true Judaism represented by the cults of Jesus, e.g., the stories of the several shifts of workmen and of the obedient and the disobedient sons.

Certain important characteristics of emerging Christianity appear in the source. Most important of these is the teaching about the church. It is significant that the most explicit consciousness of the church which is to be found in the gospels appears in the Matthean gospel, in the sections of the peculiar source. These carry the well-known Petrine interest, a distinctive feature of Matthew and of the source. The data witness the readily perceivable fact that the growth of the church was a long process which began early and was largely based upon the religious experiences of the people who were its members and its public. In the conception which appears as this gospel writer edits his source, the church is relatively highly institutionalized, even to the point that it functions in its disciplinary capacity. Evidently the materials of the source, even though it be thought that the gospel writer altered them in his editorial work, reflect the play of forces which created the church.

It is perhaps unnecessary to discuss other alleged sources in detail. To be relieved of this necessity is particularly welcome in the case of the non-Marcan materials paralleled in Matthew and Luke, e.g., the so-called Perean Document. The materials of this area are so extremely miscellaneous that it is difficult to convince oneself where a given source begins and ends. In fact, it was an open question in the minds of the authors of its basic theory whether the Perean source was one or many. However this may be, facts observable in analyzing other sources are to be found in these materials, whether they be of one or a number of sources which are not identifiable. One illustration may be cited. This concerns the bringing to convenient contexts in this area, of divers sayings the theme of which is the bearing of the believer in situations of persecution. It will be remembered that such a pericope is found in Mark (13:9-13). This interest brings into the gospel story what are, in effect, doublets of this pericope (Matt. 10:17ff, Lk. 12:11ff), and still other materials — as sayings which abound in quasi-technical terms of confession and denial. These sayings are parts of a compiled " discourse " in the source, the theme of which is the direction of the early propagandists of the cults of Jesus. They point to the expectation that opposition will be encountered.

It is thus implied that the experiences of the missionaries are the ultimate basis of the teachings which stand in the sources. An instructive detail is contributed by the saying that Jesus came, not to " throw " peace but a sword, that family dissension is to be expected, and that the final test in such a situation is whether the ultimate loyalty will be to the cult Lord. This is required, even in the shadow of the cross (Matt. 10:34–39, Lk. 12:51, 53; 14:26f). These sayings show that in the period of growth which they represent, Christianity was a disintegrating force. In other words, the scene is such a situation as that faced by Paul when he had to deal with the trend toward the breakup of families in which only one partner was a believer. When so viewed, the vividness of the gospel sources cannot be missed. The usefulness of interrogating this stage of the growth of the gospels is unquestionable.

Illustration from quite a different area of tradition may be made. The birth and infancy stories of Matthew and Luke doubtless represent later and different trends which operated in the periods of the gospel sources. Certainly they represent Hellenistic interests, for the Jewish repugnance to the idea of God generating children precluded the production of such stories in Jewish *milieux*. The development represented by the birth stories shows that the cults of Jesus in which they arose and were current were making determined bids for allegiance in gentile circles.

Perhaps of greater importance is the complementary suggestion that the processes which produced these and other similar stories (called "myths" and "legends" in form criticism) witness the interest in filling out the details of the story of Jesus' life. Undoubtedly cult interests were the basic motive of the development of biographical data in the gospels. The need of telling the story of the cult hero's life was present in circles where the cults of Jesus competed with hero and mystery cults in the Hellenistic world. It is an interest which accounts for much of the content and the form of the gospels. That the stories which it produced resemble certain elements of the apocryphal gospels should occasion no surprise. The fact merely emphasizes their Hellenistic quality and relative lateness.

These, then, are the major results which come from the search for gospel sources. Since at this point attention has been directed chiefly to the vital processes indicated by the basic interests of the materials, it is well to consider the more mechanical side, and to ask what may be said of the aggregation of the pericopes into collections and sources.

In addition to the practical effect of cult and polemical interests as impulses to the collection of materials on given themes, similarity of the form of materials of any theme doubtless caused the coherence of pericopes. For example, the identity of form probably accounts for the contiguity of the wonder stories in the early chapters of Mark, as it does for the aggregation of the polemical stories in the same area or of the parables in Mark 4. The materials were thus made readily available, and their superior availability for use in teaching may well have occasioned their grouping.

It is a fair question to ask what was the degree of fixity attained and maintained in such aggregations. It is undoubtedly significant, for example, that in his use of the Marcan source the writer of Luke-Acts made no essential change in the order of sections up to 8:3 of his work. It is often generalized from this that he treated all his source materials in this way, i.e., incorporating them in blocks without altering the order of individual pericopes. To be sure, one may not confidently assert this, since there is no way of "controlling" his procedure. On the other hand, the inference gained from the Matthean gospel is to the opposite effect. It seems from the fivefold formula at the end of the major "discourses" of this work that the evangelist combined and compiled materials from several sources to make up his own aggregations of didactic materials. Again, if the peculiar materials of Matthew are regarded as indicating a source, the processes of the gospel writer in compiling dispel the hope that the original order of the pericopes is to be seen in what the evangelist has done while incorporating them.

Similarity of form and convenience of subject matter for the use of the early Christian teacher largely account for the particular shape which the gospel materials assumed as they grew into the gospel sources. Much is to be learned from them of the religious life of the cult members. In the prolific addition to the volume of the gospel materials which they represent one sees a constant evolution of these materials as the ever enlarging horizons of expanding Christianity are observed.

It would be a mistake, however, to conclude that the growth of gospel materials into gospel sources alone will enable the student to understand all the processes of the development of Christianity. The confidence in the discovery, identification and reconstruction of gospel sources as the essential clew to the understanding of the nature of Christianity or of the growth of Christian literature is misplaced. The periods of the gospel sources are some of those in which many varying needs of the early Christians were being met, but they were periods which belong to what has aptly been called "the plastic age" of the Christian movement. The attainment of quasi-permanence awaited the formidable experiences of the gospel-making period and after.

PART TWO

THE GOSPEL-MAKING PERIOD

VI

THE GOSPELS

Christianity had a remarkable growth in the gospel-making period. The effect of its broad geographical spread was profoundly felt. To be sure, even in the days of evangelization its horizons quickly broadened, and the character of the movement was affected by this fact. But now the fullest effect of environment is to be seen. It is generally agreed that the earliest gospel reflects a Roman situation. There is some consensus that the later gospels represent Antiochene, generally Aegean, and Asian Christianity. If so, much may be learned as the gospels are studied for the light which they throw upon the emergence of the Christian movement in these centers as Christianity was consolidating.

The gospels reflect religious trends of a movement whose future, dubious in the earlier days of fortuitous evangelization, is now assured. Faced first by the problem of survival, faced next by the necessity of developing distinctive character, and constantly under the difficulty of making its way in competition with older and established cults, Christianity now met its task with confidence, neither hesitating to criticize its rivals nor shrinking from advancing its own claims. Always under the danger of suppression by the State, since its societies were without legal right to exist, the problems precipitated by this fact were faced, and out of practical experience modes of meeting them were discovered.

The non-gospel sources for the study of the gospel-making period are also highly informing. It is customary to regard "The Acts" apart from the Lucan gospel, in spite of the fact that it is the second volume of a two-volume work, and as such ought to be considered as a part of the whole which, together with the gospel section, it makes. Even when studied apart it is to be considered as a source for the study of the gospel-making period. Second, as has been pointed out, it was during this period that the Pauline letters were collected and published as a volume. Their function as a corpus, particularly in the light of the introductory covering letter, makes their information relevant for the study of the gospel-making period. Third, the so-called Epistle to the Hebrews and the Revelation of John, both products of the later years of Domitian, reflect the gospel-making period. Finally, from the same period comes at least one extra-New Testament writing; the "Epistle of the Church of Rome to the Corinthians," commonly known as 1 Clement, adds data for the study of the religious life of the Christians in the days when the gospels were being written. It is possible, also, that the work known as the *Shepherd* of Hermas should be considered as a product of the gospel-making period; a persuasive case has been made for the career of Hermas as a contemporary of Clement, and it has long been thought that parts, at least, of Hermas are as early as the gospels.

To be sure, the time limits of the gospel-making period are not to be fixed arbitrarily. Nor are they of ultimate importance. The earliest gospel was written about the year 70. But when the latest gospel was written is a question which has received various answers. It is enough to remark that the Fourth Gospel was written not much, if at all, earlier than the beginning of the second century, and not much later than 110. However, it is not important to fix a specific date for either limit. There is value in recognizing that special forces were at work in the gospel-making period, and it is the task of the present study to learn what these forces were and to observe the developments which occurred as they operated. The dividing line between the sources for the gospel-making period and the earlier period is drawn, not by date, but by the characteristics of the religious life to be observed in the sources.

The developments which occurred in the religious life during the gospel-making period were of permanent importance in the subsequent growth of Christianity, particularly in its achievement of distinctive character. It is of greater importance to study these phenomena than merely to make literary analyses of the sources which took shape in response to these formative processes. The gospels have too long been studied as though they appeared in a vacuum, or as though their appearance was the acme of Christian achievement. It cannot be too strongly urged that the gospels, like other Christian writings, were products of the religious living of the early Christians, and not themselves ends.

It has been observed that there were essential differences in the cults of Jesus in the several areas in which they were to be found. The Palestinian communities were of course the oldest, although early in the spread of the story of Jesus extra-Palestinian communities came into being. But it is unlikely that the Christian movement would ever have developed distinctive character if it had remained a Palestinian movement. For while the members of the cults of Jesus in Palestine had certain ideas and teachings which had come to them from their response to the stories of Jesus, in their religious living they seem not to have differed essentially from other Jews; they merely added certain items to current Jewish teaching. It was perhaps a decisive factor that some of the Palestinian Jews were members of Greek-speaking synagogues, for this made a bridge for the growth of a public which responded to the stories of Jesus as these were told in Greek, and thus became a step in the momentous turn which was taken when non-Jews heard and responded to the stories. It is difficult to infer whether the earliest Hellenistic communities were adjuncts of dispersion Jewish synagogues or were groups of non-Jews.[1] At all events, there were Hellenistic communities from an early date. The virility of these communities [2] is to be seen from the fact that they produced the outstanding leader that Paul proved to be, and from the fact that apart from Paul cults of Jesus early appeared at various important and strategic centers of Hellenism.

These early cults consisted of groups of people who had responded to the messages of preachers, messages which were largely Jewish in content but which brought into being, at least in the extra-Palestinian communities, types of religious living which were thoroughly gentile. It was not long until the frankly Hellenistic societies greatly outnumbered the Palestinian. Hence it is easy to see why, and not difficult to see how, Christianity developed its own characteristics in extra-Palestinian *milieux*.

However, certain elements and trends in emerging Christianity were as much out of keeping in Pauline Christianity as in Palestinian. Neither Pauline nor Palestinian Christianity was suitable soil for the growth of the gospels. It is true that in Pauline Christianity there grew up aspects of the religious life which were essential before the life which is exploited in the gospels could be given an articulated statement; e.g., freedom from observance of Torah was basic to many aspects of behavior characteristic of members of the cults of Jesus. It is likely, too, that stories of Jesus were essential in the Pauline preaching; certain emphasis upon the death and resurrection was usual in it as in the gospel stories. But the essential differences are plainer.

Palestinian Christianity had, indeed, its traditions about Jesus. But it had no impulse to write them.[3] Doubtless in these communities there was much use of orally propagated stories; it was this fact which stamped upon the materials such local color and Semitic quality as they have. But the people of these communities, relatively few in number, had a complete equipment for their moral guidance and their institutional needs. They had their synagogues, their Scripture, and their patterns for living. They awaited, calmly or eagerly, the messianic coming of Jesus. Probably this expectation marked them as different from those of their (Jewish) brethren who did not share it; perhaps at times it won for them the doubtful advantage of being " persecuted." But writing was not usual in the circles in which these believers moved as it was among the societies which were Greek in constitution; certainly not the writing of religious literature. It is well to emphasize the oral form of the stories of Jesus in the Palestinian communities.[4] This means that the likelihood of written gospels or gospel sources by and among these Palestinian believers is negligible.

In the Pauline communities, on the other hand, there was no lack of habit of writing. Writing was resorted to for every conceivable purpose, including religious propaganda. Nevertheless there was a strongly inhibitive force which militated against the writing of gospels in Pauline communities. The predilection for spiritistic behavior had a definite effect upon the attitude toward Scripture generally and toward the writing of stories of Jesus in particular. Dependence upon inspiration, normal in Paul's communities, was unfavorable to the growth of written gospels. Further, the expectation of the imminent coming of the Lord made the writing of gospels unlikely.

There was, indeed, a distinctive element in Paul's own conception of religion which does not seem to have had a counterpart in other Hellenistic circles. It is a curious fact that Paul, although he was like other early preachers in placing primary emphasis upon Jesus' death, had no interest in his life. If it be thought that Paul's letters approximate his preaching, there was no place in the preaching for reference to, much less emphasis upon, Jesus' life.

This does not seem to have been true in non-Pauline Hellenistic communities, nor, indeed, in the Palestinian. All critics unite in agreement that certain elements in the gospels go back to Palestinian communities. The conclusion is inevitable that there was something in Paul's religion which inhibited him from acquiring knowledge of, and from making use of, stories about Jesus' life. To the extent that this fact operated the Pauline communities were not those in which gospels would appear.

It is a fair question, though quite speculative, whether Paul's view in this matter controlled his communities. The work of the teacher has been cited as a possible force in bringing about collections of stories of Jesus, and thus the creation of what were in effect gospel sources. Now, the teacher was present in Paul's churches. To be sure, in these teaching was a spiritistic endowment, like prophesying, healing, and speaking in tongues. Even so, it is possible that the teacher's work may have included the telling of stories of Jesus.

But the question is more fruitfully raised when it is applied to situations subsequent to Paul's death. It is well known that not long after his death the churches in the very localities evangelized by him assumed quite different character than that of the churches seen in his letters. Christianity in these localities later became institutionalized to a point which Paul would have repudiated.

It was in some of these localities that gospels were written. Luke-Acts and the Fourth Gospel came from the very heart of the Pauline territory. They were not therefore " Pauline." Generally speaking " Paulinism " is at a discount in modern scholarship. The abandonment of eschatology in the Fourth Gospel, and the anti-Judaism of that work and of Luke-Acts, are obviously un-Pauline. These works, as the gospel literature in general, show that the gospel-making movement was uncongenial to the Pauline type of religious life.

The generally recognized Antiochene locale of the Matthean gospel is evidence of non-Pauline or of un-Pauline influence. The difference of this work from Paul's religion is commonly admitted. The Matthean gospel owes its being to entirely different impulses.

The association of the Marcan gospel with Rome accentuates the fact that non-Pauline communities produced the gospels. This was a community which Paul attempted to control in a measure, but Roman Christianity was not

Pauline. Thus there is only one conclusion possible: the gospels owe their being to forces which are new in the Christian movement; to un-Pauline and extra-Palestinian forces.

The gospels were produced because the early Christians encountered problems in their religious lives which could not be solved by primitive methods of leadership nor in primitive types of experience. They appeared because the early Christians went forward to new and untried situations in which their untrammeled freedom to experiment stood them in good stead. Long since, the problem had been settled which was precipitated by the question whether non-Jews who believed must join the Jewish race — so long since that it is hardly reflected in the gospels. Long since, the lead had been followed by which Jesus was regarded as more than an apocalyptic messiah; he was to some a hero after the pattern of Aesklepius, Herakles or Dionysus; to others he was a dying and rising savior like Osiris, Attis or Mithra. Like these gods, he had divine parentage, and during his lifetime he had noble and heroic, albeit tragic, experiences. He had done and said notable things, the stories of which might now be told and written. Long since, there had been religious societies which looked to him as their Lord and offered divine rites to him. Cult practices of these groups were of long standing, already explained and validated by legends of considerable authority.

For some time members of Christian societies had been finding that many aspects of their behavior had been influenced and affected (the modern student would say, " conditioned ") by their membership in groups. To be sure, the original purpose of accepting Jesus was to effect the " salvation " of the individual who confessed him. But the secondary results were no less important. The heavenly Jesus must secure for the believer security and welfare in this world as well as assurance of welfare in the next. Problems of this world constantly impinged upon the corporate life of the religious group. Such practical questions as the propriety of eating sacrificially slaughtered meat had been raised and answered. Other questions, some of which doubtless were forced by Jewish members or contemporaries, e.g., the right way to keep sabbath, the particular code of dietary custom, were of long standing and current relevance. Ethical questions became important as the societies became stabilized and quasi-permanent and members began to discover that fellowship in groups involved particular standards because of that fact.

Analysis of the gospel materials shows clearly that a major interest in the religious life of the early Christians was developed by the necessity of explaining certain features of their tradition. It was necessary to explain why Jesus died as he did. And, as was shown, explanations were largely derived from Scripture: it was foreordained. When it became important to relate stories of events which occurred in Jesus' life the same appeal to Scripture was made. Thus it was shown that his work as a healer was an aspect of his life which had long ago been foretold. Explanations of his nature were similarly discovered: he was the spurned building block, he was the Lord spoken of in the Psalm, he was the "boy" (i.e., the house-servant) of Isaiah's message. The same source of explanation assisted in finding reasons for specific facts, as why Jesus was born in Bethlehem, why he lived in Galilee, why he taught by parable. It made meaningful his processional entry into Jerusalem — and so on.

Why was such assiduous use made of Scripture? Obviously a number of matters explained were embarrassing, without explanation, either to Jews or to non-Jews. For example, Jesus' death as a criminal by crucifixion was disgraceful; to the Jew because one so executed was under a curse; to the non-Jew because an executed criminal was an unlikely person to be Lord of a cult. But in either case much of the embarrassment was obviated by showing, as could be done by pragmatic use of Scripture, that the event was not one of guilt but part of the foreordained plan of God. Such an explanation would have the further value to the non-Jew of being guaranteed by antiquity. The efficacy of Scripture quotation to the Jew was obvious. Its value to the Christian was enhanced when he could thus show that a given explanation was not merely the plain meaning of Scripture, but the " fulfillment " of a veiled and hidden meaning which had been concealed until the life of Jesus made it plain.

It must be seen, however, that there was a difference between the production of materials of the gospels and the writing of the gospels themselves. The processes of evangelization involved one set of problems, and these, by the enthusiastic vitality of the early Christians, had been met. The processes of definition and consolidation were of another sort. The same creative vitality met these as well. It was in the discharge of these important functions that the gospels, as distinct from their materials, were produced.

The gospels proved to be effective means for the accomplishment of the purposes for which they were intended. Indeed, it may be said that they represent a distinctively new adaptation of Christianity in the light of new problems. While they were not the sole means available during the gospel-making period (since the Pauline letters functioned institutionally and other non-gospel types of writing were then being produced) they were undoubtedly the new and distinctive achievement in the growth of Christian literature.

The point is worthy of emphasis, since one is usually prone to take the gospel form for granted. It must be brought into consciousness that the gospels represented new and radically different trends in Christianity. This can be shown clearly by pointing out that the use of the gospels was resisted. Each gospel was a local affair, whose currency was for a fairly long time limited to the neighborhood in which it was produced. Thus one gospel competed with another. Indeed, it was not until well into the second century that there was achieved the conception that the gospel was one,[5] so that each one of the gospels was, in effect, the gospel " according to " the writer of it. This conception of the fourfold gospel was an achievement comparable in its importance to the discovery that the Pauline letters when read as a whole have a message which is lacking when each is read singly. Even though this conception later succeeded in fastening itself upon common perception, it must be remembered that until this became true it was the disparate sense of each gospel which was felt.

But even when some leaders were rising to the consciousness of the gospel as such there were others who were unchangeably opposed to the use of written gospels altogether. As shall be shown later, it is this point of view which largely enables the correct use of the later books of the New Testament — the fact that after gospels came into common use there was a perpetuation of the non-gospel type of Christian writing is not only significant but of prime importance.

The point is established beyond dispute when the witness of such an early Christian leader as Papias is observed. Papias is chiefly known as the one who transmitted certain tradition about the writing of the gospels. It was he who reported the saying of the "elder" about the writing of Mark, who said that Matthew composed the oracles in "the Hebrew language," and whose ambiguity in speaking about "the elder" has so darkened counsel. It would be well if the further statements of Papias were given similar attention, particularly that he (like others) preferred "the living and the abiding voice" to what must have been the written gospels.[6] It still remains, of course, a problem as to what Papias meant by that phrase. The usual understanding is that he meant oral tradition, the paradosis. It is possible that Papias was a thoroughgoing primitive in preferring the mode of spiritistic inspiration such as had been characteristic of the Pauline communities. In any event, his statement shows that there were circles in which the use of written gospels was not common, and was, in fact, resisted. That which is new is always likely to be resisted, and the gospels were no exception to the rule.

Something of the sense of novelty in the appearance of the gospels is suggested by Bultmann's observation that while some of the gospel materials were produced and collected in Palestine the gospel as such was the creation of the Hellenistic communities. The truth of this is seen as one inspects the materials and the constitution of Mark. That this gospel differs from anything which had previously developed appears from the simple fact that no source which can be detected in it may be regarded as a gospel. What Mark represents as a whole is something entirely different from that which obtains when its contents are noted as parts. Mark illustrates the familiar axiom that the whole is more than the sum of its parts.

Further significance appears as the other gospels are studied. To what extent was the new form a norm of that which followed? Clearly the later gospel writers appreciated Mark, for they seem to have made much use of it. But when it is observed *how* Mark was used, it becomes apparent that it was no norm for the later writers to follow. Aside from the fact that each gospel relates stories of Jesus, giving major attention to his death, exceptions rather than generalizations are the rule. The Matthean gospel prefaces a genealogy and a story of Jesus' birth and completely alters the story of Jesus by giving primary attention to what Jesus taught, presenting his materials in extensive discourses. When Luke-Acts is, as it should be, viewed as a whole, the dissimilarity which is emphasized by the current " Proto-Luke " theory pales into insignificance as the Marcan contribution to Luke-Acts is placed in its true perspective. The Fourth Gospel is closer to Mark than is Luke-Acts. Still farther from the Marcan norm are the apocryphal gospels. One must conclude that the writer of Mark did indeed create something new, but this new thing in the hands of others became a very fluid medium.

The writer of Mark must then be regarded as a remarkable innovator. He was, of course, familiar with a large fund of tradition about Jesus, things which Jesus had " said," and with remarkably fine didactic narratives which had already become known as " parables," as well as stories of what Jesus "did" — the most distinctive feature of his own work. It is probable that some of these had assumed aggregate form before they came to his hand. But in the main the materials were thoroughly disparate and miscellaneous. The gospel writer made a distinctive contribution when he saw the advantage to be gained by choosing from the total fund the materials which he regarded as useful for his purpose, assembling these materials, organizing them according to the motifs [7] and patterns which he had developed, thus making of these parts the remarkable whole which is the earliest gospel.

To be sure, some steps in the process were simple. The author had merely to add conventional phrases to individual stories, such as "and he said to them," "and they came to . . ," "and they went . . ," etc., and to place them in narrative context. However, his work was not merely that of mechanically placing where he chose the individual pericopes of his gospel. The most notable thing about the earliest gospel is that it is conceived according to plan: the author is presenting the tragic story of Jesus to readers for its helpfulness in their religious lives. The important elements are equally involved: the needs of their religious lives, and the author's conception of the tragic story. [8]

He tells the story of Jesus as a spirit-endowed person, whose life of great deeds was most beneficent in its service to his fellows, not the least of whose gifts to them was the example of a nobly austere religious life. The major feature of this, although there is the use of Jewish messianic figures, is the deliberately accepted role of the persecuted hero. The high point of the Marcan narrative is the recognition scene in which the messianic identification is made, only to be followed by three cumulatively effective announcements of the tragic hero's death; the major theme is then worked out in the relatively extensive story of the self-accepted way of the cross. It is highly probable that the fundamental conception of this gospel was valuable as a practical illustration for those whose life must perforce be austere because it was lived under the constant shadow of potential persecution.

It is likely that the other gospels were written with similar motivation and according to similar processes. Their writers, too, collected chosen materials from the total fund which they knew and arranged them according to particular purposes.

The writer called "Matthew" approximates the great bulk of the materials which Mark used. In the main he supplemented these by compiling extensive discourses, which he introduced at convenient places in the outline maintained in Mark. However, he sometimes incorporated sources without editing away certain of their characteristics, even though some of these were inconsistent with certain of his favorite ideas. Broadly speaking, the author of the Matthean gospel labors to picture Jesus as a second Moses, the giver of God's true Law. He thus presents the religion which it was his purpose to propagate as a new law. Naturally this involved its contrast with the old Law, i.e., Judaism. Consequently there is much anti-Jewish polemic in Matthew. It is strange, since this is so apparent, that Matthew has so long been regarded as fundamentally Jewish. It is only when certain statements are emphasized by themselves that anything particularly Jewish appears in Matthew. This gospel says, for example, that Jesus was sent only to Jews. But when this and the few other such items are viewed according to the modern emphasis upon the individual pericopes, when these are counterbalanced by plainly Hellenistic elements, and when they are further seen to be elements of sources from which inconsistencies have not been edited away, no basis remains for the judgment that Matthew is a Jewish gospel.

Essential anti-Judaism is seen plainly in the Matthean gospel in its contrast between the religious attitudes and acts deemed by its author[9] to be right and those of "the hypocrites of the synagogues," the "scribes and Pharisees," and, as they are once (28:15) astonishingly called, "the Jews." It is hardly less apparent as the theme of displacement is worked out in several parables (the several shifts of workers, 20:1–16; the two sons, 21:28–32; the unworthy tenants, 21:33–44; the impressed guests, 22:1–14). Much of the substance of these materials is theological, but actual conditions of the religious life may also be seen. What is especially to be noted is that while Jewish legalism is severely criticized, the religion which the gospel propagates is itself definitely legalistic.

However, Jewish legalism is not the only religious attitude criticized by the writer of Matthew. Non-Jewish religionists are not less sharply pilloried ("After such things as these the gentiles seek," ". . . the gentiles . . . do not be like them," 6:32, 7). The Matthean gospel represents a group independent both of Jewish and gentile cults.

All this is written plainly over the Matthean gospel. The really notable aspect of the work is its didactic content. This is the important feature, not merely as an aspect of structure, but as the didactic is viewed functionally. This approach exhibits the status of the Christian movement which is indicated by the significance of its ethical teaching. In the didactic of Matthew one may observe several elements of the process by which the religious life of the community has become, or is becoming, "Christian." Its members now have their own ways of celebrating cult services, or performing moral-religious acts of devotion, liturgy and charity, and it is one of the major purposes of the gospel writer similarly to articulate standards of behavior which may likewise characterize the people of the cult. Thus, both in relation to rival religions and in the achievement of the religious life of individuals of this group, "Christian" ways of life have become distinctive.

To be sure, it is the intellectual conviction of the gospel writer that his group thus realizes the essential features of true Judaism. This is doubtless why he presents his religion as law. Likewise he presents Jesus as God's Anointed, as "King of the Jews," and assiduously he cites Jewish Scripture for its evidential value. However, he consistently maintains an objective attitude toward Judaism. He causes Jesus to warn his followers against the leaven, which he takes pains to define as the teaching of "the Pharisees and the Sadducees"—in effect, of Judaism. In the same discourse in which he causes Jesus to pronounce a validation of Pharisaic teaching (23:3), apparently without noting the contradiction of this with the warning against Jewish teaching, he no less strictly makes the point that the Jewish teachers fail to do what they teach.

The matter is put positively, also. Jesus is moved to pity as he considers the people as unshepherded sheep. He has a mission for Galilee of the nations. He finds the appeal of a Greek woman to be irresistible. The limitation of missionary work to Jews is merely a prelude to a world-wide mission in which all of the nations shall be evangelized. One of the most striking of the didactic pericopes pictures the judgment of all the nations; this does not necessarily imply a universalism, but significantly it includes more than Jews. Perhaps most explicit of all is the moral which is drawn as the evangelist edits the parable, found in Mark and Luke also, of the unworthy tenants. For he causes Jesus to say: " The kingdom of heaven shall be taken away from you and shall be given to a nation which shall bring forth its fruit." These elements make it perfectly plain that the Matthean gospel represents a religion which, while it utilizes certain values of Judaism, is inclusive of non-Jews and now bids for reception by any and all who may be interested. It is a religion which is now articulating its own ethic. It retains a vivid apocalypticism in its teaching, but in its actual life the cult is practically at home in this world.

The Matthean gospel is interested in integrating emerging Christianity within the Roman State. This interest had some expression in the earliest gospel. But the greater abundance of persecution sayings shows that this gospel goes much farther than does the Marcan. Some of these sayings are paralleled in Mark, but here they are used as doublets in other contexts. Others are independent. The attitude represented in them is far from quiescent. This gospel proposes that its religion shall be aggressively promulgated even though State opposition is incurred.

In fine, the religion which is promoted by the Gospel of Matthew is a virile religion, a religion which is far from its infancy. It is capable of consciously deriving values from older religions, as well as vigorously maintaining its own values against theirs in polemic. It is a religion which has taken over many values from its competitors, not hesitating to assimilate and adapt elements of the Graeco-Roman religions. The obvious example of this is, of course, its incorporation of a story of Jesus' birth of a virgin by miraculous conception. What is of the highest importance is that what this religion has become, by growth from its slender beginnings, by assimilation and by appropriation, is a religion with its own individuality.

It has been sufficiently urged that in studying Luke-Acts the two volumes should be used as parts of a whole, thus overcoming the injury which the work suffered by its separation into two books, which are placed, both in manuscripts and in printed New Testaments, without even the advantage of juxtaposition. The present study will practice the principle of studying Luke-Acts as a unit.

So viewed, Luke-Acts is seen to tell a story which begins with items about John as Jesus' forerunner and ends only with Paul's pronouncement in Rome that the claims of Judaism have been canceled in favor of the status of non-Jewish believers. The purpose of the writer relates to this entire story. It is a great loss when attention is allowed to drop with the story of the raising of Jesus from the dead; the story does not end, nor should it be interrupted, here. The purpose of Luke-Acts *as a whole* must be apprehended.[10]

It may be remarked that the processes of the writing of Luke-Acts were the same throughout the two volumes.[11] The Acts section, no less than the gospel section, was produced by the selection and use of so and so many pericopes which had arisen as had the gospel materials. Indeed, many phenomena found in the gospels are present in the second

volume of Luke-Acts: parallel sections which can be exhibited in "harmonized" parallel columns (e.g., the three accounts of Paul's "conversion"), the occurrence of doublet
forms of the same story (Peter and the magus, Paul and
Elymas), use of sources (a letter, the "we sources"),[12] and
the compilation of discourses. Items effecting the purpose of
the whole are found in each part, e.g., Jesus and Paul are
pictured as ideal "witnesses" (or martyrs), particularly in
their several "trials." Special interests appear in both sections (foreigners, money, women, attitude toward the State).
Doubtless the bulk of materials available to the writer was
less in composing the Acts section than for the gospel section, but the processes of their use were essentially the same.

When Luke-Acts is studied as the product of the gospel-
making period it exhibits emerging Christianity (one might,
indeed, speak of Christianity without committing an anachronism) as not only thoroughly spread in the Graeco-Roman
world, but as integrated into this world. It is a religion of
such well-developed character that it unhesitatingly bids for
general acceptance and tacitly claims legitimization by the
State. In fact, it is a major element of the purpose of Luke-
Acts to show that Christianity, having of right succeeded
to all the privileges of Judaism, is entitled thereby to all the
benefits of an allowed religion. Such a conception indicates
a complete at-homeness in this world, a result of a now long
continued growth and a definitely accomplished solidarity.
It is significant that the Acts section reports that at Antioch
the disciples had come to be called Christians. The adherents of the cult had achieved a name.

The traditions articulated in Luke-Acts, and appearing
there only, greatly enrich the fund of information about

early Christianity. Significantly, these materials indicate an extensive adaptation to gentile environment. Christianity is presented, even in the " teaching of Jesus," as a salvation cult. The author is fond of picturing in both sections episodes in which gentiles appear as heroes. Of greater importance is the fact that the articulation of moral and ethical patterns is not only advanced in degree and fuller in content, but is with reference to particular interests. For example, Luke-Acts is especially interested in the problems of wealth and poverty, and is characterized by still other humanitarian interests.

The major characteristic of Luke-Acts is that its story is conceived as a great whole, so that it proceeds from a grand perspective. It is of much significance that the narrative begins, not with a story of the birth of Jesus, but with a story of the miraculous conception and miraculously attended birth of John as Jesus' forerunner. The purpose of this was to place the story of Jesus within Judaism, so as subtly to subordinate Judaism to Christianity. In line with this the story has for its main trend the report of Christianity's expansion in the Graeco-Roman world, culminating with Paul's presentation of it in Rome. This involves a studied transference of the values and rights of Judaism to Christianity. It is interesting that although they differ in their ways of doing it, both Luke-Acts and Matthew shape their materials with reference to the displacement of Judaism in favor of Christianity. Again, while the manner and the degree of their reflection of gentile interests differ, both exhibit Christianity in competition with gentile, as well as with Jewish rivals. However, Luke-Acts much the more plainly reflects contacts with the State. The evidence of this, naturally, is more abundant in the Acts section, but it is found in both parts.

In comparison with the Matthean gospel, Luke-Acts gives less attention to didactic materials relating to behavior. It must not be thought that Luke-Acts was less interested in these matters. Many of the data grouped by Matthew into great discourses appear in different distribution in the gospel section of Luke-Acts. But the Acts section assumes the same ethical attitudes. There was purpose in these ways of treating materials. For example, the Fourth Gospel is not deficient in its ethical standard; the more immediate purpose which led its writer to subordinate the practical to the speculative and transcendental interests explains his apparent lack of interest in ethical teaching.

When the Christianity of the gospel-making period receives articulation in the latest gospel, its communal life is plainly to be observed, even though it is not a primary purpose of the work to exhibit it. The corporate development of the movement is easy to see, especially as it is placed in utter antithesis to Judaism. Between Judaism and the Christianity of the Fourth Gospel there is an impassable breach. The fact is willingly accepted. The gospel writer tells the story of Jesus as though the antithesis had been current in Jesus' day; Jesus is caused to speak for the group as against the Jews, " We speak of what we know, but you [the word is plural] do not receive our testimony "; he is caused to refer, like Pilate, to " your (*sic*) law."

But more significant is the fact that the greatest single distinctive aspect of the Fourth Gospel, the long discourse of chapters 14–17, has for its object the guidance of the New Community. When the full force of this is seen, the details fall into place. It is explained that Jesus must go away, but that his followers must go on without him; when he goes away the Paraclete will come and remain with them. They are told that trouble and persecution will come, but that the Paraclete will be their present defender. The world will be hostile, but Jesus has overcome the world. Most important is that the followers of Jesus must be in unity; they must be one. Even though it is only in the Matthean gospel that the word " church " occurs, the conception is to be observed in the Fourth Gospel. Indeed, the conception is an advanced one, as is patently indicated in the ideal of unity. The very terminology requires one to compare the conception of the church in " Ephesians." The wide outreach of the New Community is more than merely suggested in the figure of the sheep in other folds who must be brought into this fold; it is explicit when Jesus is caused to pray not only for his immediate followers but for those who believe through their word. Finally, the pronouncement of blessing upon those who believe without having seen Jesus makes the point unmistakable. The corporate achievement of Christianity is plainly to be seen in the Fourth Gospel.

The same character appears in the fact that constantly elements are assumed without logical or narrative consistency. For example, the cult interests are always important, but they are not necessarily treated with reference to their rise or their authentication by Jesus. The story of Jesus multiplying food, one of the points at which the Fourth Gospel coincides with the synoptics, is the peg upon which to hang a discourse. The theme of the discourse is the necessity of eating the body and drinking the blood of Jesus, which requires the sacrament of the Lord's supper to make it intelligible. But as they stand they lack narrative consistency. This is but one example of a frequently recurring phenomenon. Of the same sort is the fact that the death of Jesus is in view from the beginning of the story. Again, the antithesis between the Christian movement and Judaism is treated as though it had obtained during Jesus' lifetime. So, too, the coming of the Paraclete is carefully prepared for during his lifetime. Unquestionably the Fourth Gospel reflects much of the status of the Christian movement at the time of its writing, more, certainly, than it reflects of the actual situations of its dramatic date. It is, as it were, a great work of art whose logic is in such categories as preserve these elements from being incongruities.

The more obvious characteristics which exhibit the religious life pictured by the Fourth Gospel are those which are really metaphysical. These are carried by a highly individual terminology. That they are thoroughly Hellenistic hardly needs to be pointed out. They show that Christianity is thoroughly at home in the Greek world, so that the story of Jesus may be recast in terms which are in obvious contrast to even that degree of Palestinian local color which is preserved in the other gospels. It should not be thought that they indicate a high intellectual achievement; the Fourth Gospel does not exploit a philosophy. To be sure, it represents a contrast with the synoptic gospels in a certain degree of intellectualization. But it is a simple intellectualization. The gospel was written to prove something. Thus the intellectualization of the Fourth Gospel is one which involves belief. Consequently its message is with reference to belief, sin and justness; status is determined merely by belief, otherwise involving moral relations not at all.

Such phenomena show that in the writing of the Fourth Gospel some essentially different processes were utilized. Here the stories of Jesus are not those in whose oral transmission the form is given by naïve repetition; in these the form is achieved through reflection. Only a few of the stories coincide with the synoptic gospel cycles. The major part, more suitable to the symbolic effect of the discourses attached to them, have come into the fund of new materials. Even the story of the Passion is given individual turn in the interest of reflection and symbolic interpretation, as is shown by the story which causes the death of Jesus to coincide with the slaying of the Passover victim.

It is true that the synoptic gospels also use stories for pragmatic effect. But here there is an obvious maturity; an atmosphere in the narrative suggests that there is no immediacy in the situations ostensibly related. The stories are types, important for the interpretative words which accompany them. It is a legitimate inference that the maturity is not merely that of the gospel; it is of Christianity. The latest gospel, like the earliest and all others, reflects the contemporary status which emerging Christianity has attained in its time and place.

VII

THE NON-GOSPEL LITERATURE OF THE
GOSPEL-MAKING PERIOD

It is of prime importance to remember that writings of other than the gospel form were produced by the early Christians during the gospel-making period. The matter is important, if for no other reason than to correct the misapprehension caused by the common notion that the gospels were regarded by the early Christians as they are by the modern, to correct the erroneous impression that they were appreciated above all else. The correct viewpoint must be reiterated until it is firmly in the student's consciousness: the gospels were one form of writing developed by the early Christians, but they were one form only; before them were examples of another type and beside them were examples of other types, while after them many writings of the non-gospel variety were produced.

There are four non-gospel writings of the gospel-making period which furnish important information of the religious life of the early Christians. The first, coming after the appearance of Luke-Acts and closely dependent upon its appearance, is the collection for institutional use of Paul's letters.[1] It was a remarkable discovery, made by some otherwise unknown religious leader, that Paul's letters have a different message when they are read together than they have when each is read singly as a message to an individual church. Together they have a message for all the churches, or, indeed, for the " Church."

To be sure, much lies back of this remarkable discovery. First, the movement of which Paul was a great, although not the first nor the sole representative, had developed in certain respects as Paul would have approved. He had no hesitation in taking his message to non-Jews, and welcomed them into fellowship when they believed without requiring them to become Jews. Now the gentile character of Christianity was an obvious feature. But such representation as the movement had had among Jews, particularly in Palestine, had dwindled until the number of Jewish believers was inconsiderable and their influence narrowed and greatly lessened.

Second, as has been shown, Christianity had developed its own characteristics. It had its own customs, moral patterns, ethical standards, and its own ecclesiastical constitution as well. It had a " Church " consciousness. Not merely the use of the word in the Matthean gospel, but the development of the theme of the guidance of the New Community in the Fourth Gospel, and most particularly the plea in this work for unity — all these suggest explicitly the similar conception in the so-called Letter to the Ephesians, the introductory covering letter to the collected epistles of Paul.

Third, the collection of Paul's letters and their use as a group indicates what has been observed elsewhere: the growth of the institutional equipment in Christianity. This is in no sense to suggest that the collected use of Paul's letters gave them authority as Scripture. They were, none the less, part of the institutional equipment of such churches as possessed copies.

It is in the advancement of the corporate sense of the

Christian societies that the particular standpoint of the collector of Paul's letters is to be seen. Two features are apparent. He has developed a formulation of teaching which is essentially theological: he presents the developments which have led to the present status of the Christian movement as divinely ordered, so that it was inevitable that everything occur as it has. He has formulated an explanation of Jesus which is comparable in the degree of its advance, in distinction from the more primitive reflections found in the letters. He understands Jesus' nature with reference to the unfolding of divinely controlled purposes. Second, he articulates a conception of the church as an institution. This conception has several instructive features. It is not merely that there is a " high ecclesiology " in " Ephesians." It is that the conception goes far beyond anything to be found in Paul. The apparent paradox is to be understood in the fact that the collector of Paul's letters has articulated this conception as the result of reflection upon the entire religious point of view he has encountered in the letters which he herewith issues for the instruction of the whole church.

Paul does not seem to have had any consciousness of " the Church." He was acutely conscious of the churches. The genius who published his letters as a book presents in his introductory letter the generalization which came to him as a gentile Christian who had read and been deeply influenced by the letters. He has fundamental sympathy with Paul's conception of religion, and lives a type of religious life which was akin to that of the Pauline communities, although, of course, it differed in such detail as was necessitated by the more complex situations of the current Christian communities.

It is a challenging fact that the perception of the church in " Ephesians " is best understood when it is observed in the light of the status of Christianity as it is seen in the Fourth Gospel. As in this work, the necessity for unity is forced in large part by the presence of sectaries — believers must now have a rational understanding, and not be blown about by every wind of teaching. But most strikingly of all, although it was perhaps written a few years earlier than the Fourth Gospel, the introductory letter has an attitude toward the relation of Jews and non-Jews which goes far beyond that of the latest work of the gospel-making period. Indeed, the attitude toward this question is a theoretical one. The de-cided negative in the attitude of the Fourth Gospel is coun-terbalanced by the coolly reflective explanation that it was part of the effect of Christ that the wall between Jew and non-Jew was broken down, the Law abolished, and the two groups brought together in mystical union with Christ. The fundamental element is very like Paul's attitude, but the conclusion is hardly Paul's! For there is no reason to con-clude that this beautiful relationship ever obtained. The fact is reflected plainly by the Fourth Gospel and Luke-Acts; " Ephesians " presents an abstraction of what might have ob-tained, had the hopes of Paul been realized.

It is instructive, also, to use Luke-Acts as a perspective for the study of "Ephesians." Much of what it has and is re-quires Luke-Acts for its very being. For example, the pic-ture of Paul (pseudonymously depicted), the prisoner for the Lord's sake, the prisoner for the sake of the non-Jews, the preacher *par excellence* to the non-Jews, and the Paul who is one with the other apostles, missionaries and teachers. But whereas Luke-Acts pictures Paul as finally wearied of giving "the Jews" another opportunity and another and another, pronouncing their doom and figuratively opening the door to the gentiles, "Ephesians" sees the house filled as the door has long been opened. Thus there is no need longer to hold the point against the Jews. Now the resultant constitution of the group can be called "the commonwealth of Israel" — again, the fundamental element is Paul's, but the reality is a development far removed from him.

The Christianity of "Ephesians" is that of a salvation cult which is so similar to the mystery cults that the parallelism goes far beyond mere terminology. The cult myth is understood as a divine mystery. Its content now included a *decensus ad infernum* (4:8–10). Cult practice is so fully developed that ritual elements are referred to and liturgy is actually quoted in snatches of hymns.

The practical problems reflected are in line with this status. The contrast is emphasized between what the cult members used to be and what they must be now (which, presumably, was not exactly what they were). They used to live as pagans; now they must live lives of strict propriety. In all this the author is proceeding from a Pauline basis in a later situation. Thus it is in keeping that he greatly expands the table of household duties which he found in Colossians. His expansion is instructive as indicating the more complex situations of the Christian homes of his day. Significantly, he can use the church as sanction for the pattern of the proper relationship between married people. It is a great secret, he says, but he cleverly applies it, no doubt with effect.

The new elements in Christianity which are reflected in the collected letters of Paul are not merely the items of the so-called letter to the Ephesians. The most important new feature is the fact that when published together they have a message for the whole church. This is different from the effect which accrues when each is read to observe its message to the church to which it was addressed. "Ephesians" merely generalizes this and sets forth the themes of the several letters, as an overture announces the *motifs* of the music drama. Inevitably specific purposes of separate letters are submerged as new times and places have had their effect, e.g., the introductory letter does not suggest that ecstatic behavior was practiced or desired. But great religious and theological generalizations appear in the restatement of Paul's messages for the church of a new day.

On the physical side the collector, having assembled such letters as it was possible for him to find, proceeded by arranging them in desirable form and subjecting them to such editing as he considered necessary. The order of the letters presents interesting problems; doubtless this editor, like the Marcionite of whose work something may be learned,[2] arranged the letters in the order of their extent or bulk, by way of exception placing (so the hypothesis supposes) "Ephesians" at the beginning as the introductory covering letter. But it is uncertain just how the order by size was determined.[3] Certain phenomena in Romans, for example, suggest that this letter existed in more than one form, and therefore in differing lengths.[4] Was it the first collector who appended what is now chapter 16 of Romans to that letter?[5] Was it he who "edited" the fragments of our 2 Corinthians into the canonical letter? If so, was it he, actuated by a delicate sense of fitness, who exscinded more or less extensive sections from the "bitter letter"? Probably it was he who placed the familiar doxology at the end of the Corinthian correspondence, since 2 Corinthians probably formed the end of the first of the two rolls required by the corpus. What further editorial work did he do? This is, obviously, a speculative question which admits of no answer. However, it is well to remember that the text of the Pauline letters reached its first fixation only toward the end of the first century.

There are three additional sources for the study of the religious life in the gospel-making period. One is a homily which has been denominated an "epistle," perhaps because of the slight editorial work which was done upon it in supplying a quasi-epistolary conclusion. One is a mosaic of apocalyptic materials, much of which is Jewish, but the whole greatly modified by the presence of certain Hellenistic elements which more than balance the Jewish aspects, and by a prefatory collection of letters to seven churches together with a general introductory letter to all the churches. The third is an "epistle" from the Roman church to the church at Corinth, commonly known as First Clement, since it was written by one Clement of Rome. These writings, like the gospels, present information of the gospel-making period, during which they were written.

Specific impulse from the political stress which was seen in the gospels was the effective cause of the appearance of these three writings. Political stress was fairly constant in the time when all the sources of the gospel-making period were produced. Naturally, as the Christian consciousness developed during the decades when the gospel materials were taking shape, the problems of the right attitude toward the State became more acute. It is regrettable that lack of definite information inhibits the detailed chronicle of the processes by which the characteristic attitudes took shape. There are traditions, but not only do these require critical scrutiny, but the data from non-Christian sources are scanty and dubious. At all events, the impact of pressure from the State was being felt while the writings of the gospel-making period were taking shape; this is to be seen in the gospel traditions, these non-gospel writings of the period, and in Josephus [6] and the Ezra-apocalypse (not to mention the Christian form of the Ascension of Isaiah).

The difficulty of determining a specific situation for the so-called Epistle to the Hebrews accounts for the fact that studies of this document are usually far below the quality of scholarly work done upon other Christian sources. Nowhere does the feebleness of quality appear more plainly than in the failure to take into account the religious life exhibited. There is a growing consensus that Hebrews reflects the persecution of Domitian, and, what is of prime importance, to regard it in connection with 1 Clement.[7] The common judgment that it also reflects Alexandrian culture also acts to hinder its study as a source of knowledge of the religious life, since so little is known of Alexandrian Christianity. The day is past, of course, when it is thought that the "Epistle" was written "to the Hebrews."[8] There is general willingness to abandon the tradition of Pauline authorship.

The keys to the understanding of Hebrews, and to its proper use as a source, are three. First, a situation appears when it is viewed in relation to the Domitianic persecution,[9] so that its information is added to that of Revelation and 1 Clement. Second, the student is advantaged when he regards the work as a homily.[10] Third, its character is largely understood when it is observed that the work is largely shaped by the processes of the religious life which were characteristic of Alexandria.

With reference to its integration into Alexandrian life, a

number of features are to be noted. Most important is the intellectualism of Alexandrian theology and the point of view of Hebrews. The work cannot be understood until it is perceived that its argument is highly academic. For example, its use of illustrations from Judaism is in no sense relevant to the actual aspects of current Jewish life; the long dissertation on the tent in the desert proves this, as does the reference to the Temple, which institution did not exist at the time the document was written. Again, the rhetoric of the homily points to Alexandria, and is, as the best commentaries show, chiefly to be illustrated from Alexandrian examples. Most plainly of all, the Septuagint quotations point to Alexandria.

This does not necessarily mean that Hebrews was written in Alexandria. Information of first century Christianity in Alexandria is too scant to permit such an affirmation. All that can be said with any probability is that Hebrews is an address, chiefly concerned with strengthening the morale of Christians in a situation of persecution, the address made by a Christian leader whose literary gift was strongly conditioned by Alexandrian thought and speech.

Such a generalization does, however, satisfy the necessities. Christianity seems to have attained an intellectualization first in Alexandria. Such as it was, it was articulated largely with reference to an abstract conception of Judaism. This, in turn, was principally derived from a certain manner of using the Greek translation of Jewish Scripture. Why these processes first occurred there it is difficult to determine. The fact, however, remains. The " Preaching of Peter "[11] has been characterized as the beginning of Christian apologetic. It is reflected in the writings of Alexandrian leaders and appears to have been Alexandrian; it, too, is chiefly occupied by statements in which just such an abstract conception of Judaism appears as is found in Hebrews. The so-called Epistle of Barnabas, likewise Alexandrian in character, is concerned with the defense of Christianity as a new law; its points are made by similar use of the Septuagint.

Other aspects of Christian apologetic suggest what forces acted to precipitate the defensive impulse. The writings of Justin furnish an example. Here there are two themes: Christianity is better than Judaism and better than the various gentile cults; Christianity deserves recognition by the State. It has been shown that these same elements are implicit in the gospels and are all but explicit in Luke-Acts. They are to be found in the gospels in varying degrees: in the Fourth Gospel Christianity's superiority to Judaism appears as obvious, while in Luke-Acts the case with reference to the State is urged. In Justin's *Apology* and its supplement the latter theme dominates, while in the *Dialogue with Trypho* the former is primary.

It was these two interests which caused Christianity's early articulation of its claims. Now, both these interests are to be found in Hebrews. It urges that the cult of Jesus is better than Judaism, developing the point by using literary and dialectic methods. Likewise, but with more practical tone, it gives reasons why the cult member's loyalty must be to Jesus rather than to the State. Obviously the intellectual level of this argument is lower than that of the former. This might be expected, in view of its earlier date and the greater pressure of the theme of tension with the State.

When Hebrews is thus viewed it is perhaps not surprising that the apologetic document is a homily. For it is the voice of Christian leadership which rings in Hebrews. It is an eloquent voice, able to phrase its claims with elegance of idiom and sonority of period. It is a voice lifted in demand, not in plea, that communities in places of responsibility must lead in a time of crisis. It is directly argued that those addressed used to be heroic and must be heroic now. This part of the message, at least, is not academic.

Hebrews is valuable for showing that Christianity in this time and place has secured for itself spokesmen who are not representative of the rather crude level of culture indicated by the gospel materials. The culture of this leader exceeds that suggested by the uneven literary quality of Luke-Acts. Here is a spokesman who brings to Christianity's service intellectual ability and achievement gained by study of Alexandrian literature.

Problems formerly handled purely practically by earlier leaders are treated here with a stylized rhetoric and a generalized thoughtfulness which befit a cultured leadership. Pressing problems are treated with elegance of expression. The error in the usual study of Hebrews comes when the elegance, the style, and the seeming abstractness are allowed to detract attention from the actual situation which was important to the author of the written address. The correct proportioning of these aspects should enable the discovery of that crisis which brought forth a considerable literature — a literature which is more considerable than is generally supposed.

The situation was one of pressure in which the persons addressed have been placed. Their group has faced such a situation before, at that time with high credit. Now it is feared that they are in danger of disintegration because of the lack of aggressive, courageous and informed leadership. The ultimate purpose of Hebrews is to urge the group addressed to rise to the occasion.

What was the occasion? Who were the people addressed? It may be urged that the answer to these questions is found when the evident relation of Hebrews and 1 Clement are taken as the essential clew, and 1 Clement is seen to have been called forth by Hebrews. This suggests that the homily was addressed to a Roman group, which is thus being urged to equal the heroism with which an earlier Roman group met "persecution." The simple meaning would then be that the earlier "persecution" was that terrible time when Nero put so many Christians to torture and death. The further point would then appear that 1 Clement was written to show (among other things) that the Roman congregation has not failed, but has been adequate to everything which presented itself.

These suggestions have long been placed before scholars for their consideration. It has been argued that the Domitianic "persecution" called forth a large complex of Christian writing, including not only Hebrews and 1 Clement, but also Revelation, 1 Peter and Luke-Acts; as well as Josephus' *Antiquities* and 4 Ezra by Jewish writers. This study treats 1 Peter differently, as shall appear. But without it the volume of Christian writing called forth by the stress of Domitian's suppression is astonishing. It shows conclusively that political situations were strongly operative in stimulating Christian leaders to action.

Each of these writings exhibits a leader or leaders attempting to deal practically with whatever problems are precipitated by strained relations between Christians and the State.

Each is the work of a leader or a group who felt that the people of the community were under persecution or in danger of it, and who saw that something must be done if the situation was to be met with a degree of success. Different leaders attempted different expedients. Some of these may be observed in the several writings.

As has been shown elsewhere, the entire story of Christianity's success in meeting the problems of persecution may be told, and the processes observed in detail. For the present purpose all that needs to be said is that writing was one method of exerting control.[12]   Certain forms of writing became conventional. The most characteristic, and in some ways the most interesting, of these literary types was the martyrology. This did not, of course, have its rise until the experience of persecution had become familiar. It could not be expected that examples would obtain in the Domitianic period. In this situation, as was shown, the Christians produced no less than four types of writing. Luke-Acts is an apologetic narrative of the story of Jesus and of the wide expansion of Christianity. Hebrews is a written homily; Revelation is a modified apocalypse; 1 Clement is an epistle. Doubtless these examples of the several forms were produced spontaneously, with little premeditation. The literary forms had interesting later development. The Epistle remained in use as a form of persecution literature. The apologetic telling of Christianity's growth grew into the formal Apology. The Homily whose theme was that of exhortation to heroic behavior in persecution appeared also later; interestingly enough, one of the greatest of them was another Alexandrian document, Origen's *Exhortation to Martyrdom*. The Apocalypse was abandoned in favor of the Martyrology.

With this perspective it is not difficult to place the writings
of the Domitianic suppression into relation with their backgrounds. It will not be regarded as strange if they are found
to contain elements which are not immediately typical. For
example, the problems of control in persecution are not the
only ones addressed in 1 Clement. This long work contains
many themes. The data of persecution account for several
"chapters" toward the beginning. Paul and Peter are cele-
brated as models in language which strongly suggests the use
of Luke-Acts. The reflections of Hebrews are plain in the
persecution sections and elsewhere; the reactions of the Roman church to the challenge of Hebrews are clearly set forth.
But aside from persecution, a major purpose in 1 Clement is
the attempt of the Roman church to assert control over the
Corinthians in some matters of official church organization.
The Roman form of the ministry is asserted as against the
Eastern form, i.e., there must be separate orders of deacons,
elders and bishops, not merely two orders. Throughout
there is extensive use of Scripture, of course the Greek translation of Jewish writings. Sometimes a quotation occupies
an entire section of text; the writer's command of Scripture
(presumably quoted from memory) is amazing. There is
a long written prayer. Occasionally there is an unmistakable
ring of other Christian writings, including Pauline letters
and gospels. There are citations which appear like gospel
sayings but which do not correspond to our written gospels.
These used to be regarded as survivals of the oral tradition.
They may now be viewed as excerpts from gospel pericopes
in forms which came to the writer of the Epistle, differing
from the forms which were known to the gospel writers.
First Clement shows in its range of interests that the Roman

church speaks with ready acceptance of the challenge of Hebrews, meeting its situation with dignity and (it may be presumed) with success. While the letter does not have the literary excellence which is found in Hebrews, on the whole it is written in Greek of good quality.

The Revelation of John also exhibits varieties of interests and departures from type. In the first place, unlike Jewish apocalypses, it is presented in the name of its seer, without the fiction of pseudonymity. As has been mentioned, it begins with a non-apocalyptic letter group. While everything in this section links with the remainder of the book in style and diction, certain peculiar Hellenistic qualities appear in the letter section. Most important is the fact that individualism [13] of address is uppermost here, the refrain of the letters is an appeal " to him who conquers," even though the letters are addressed to church groups.

In the apocalyptic materials more properly speaking there are further modifications of the apocalyptic form. The emphasis upon the distinction of the martyrs is an important illustration.[14] Their praise is sounded repeatedly in tones which are much more similar to Hellenistic models than to typical Jewish apocalypses. If the Johannine apocalypse is compared, point by point, with the contemporaneous 4 Ezra, this difference becomes apparent. On the other hand, parallels of this phenomenon in Jewish writings are found only in those which are patently Hellenistic, e.g., 2 and 4 Maccabees.

Another instance is the use of Hellenistic literary forms. It is an interesting fact, the details of which cannot be exhibited here, that a number of the conventional elements of the Greek drama are to be observed in the *mise en scène* of

Revelation. For example, the twenty-four old men, in number and function, parallel the chorus of the drama. The Greek aspects of the cosmic pageantry of the apocalypse are obvious. In content and in form the supposedly Jewish Revelation is importantly modified by Hellenistic factors.

To be sure, it is probable that the writer of the book proceeded by using a number of sources which were fundamentally Jewish. Doubtless the cryptogram based upon the number 666 is Jewish in all respects, including its being based upon Semitic numerals.[15] A thorough analysis of Revelation abundantly shows its author's familiarity with and dependence upon a wide range of apocalyptic literature, much of which came to him through Jewish sources.[16] It was because the religious life of the group which he represented had become so thoroughly integrated in the Roman world that he modified his materials as he did. Indeed, John's revelation is no mere mosaic of apocalyptic sources. This is shown not merely by the prefacing of the apocalypse by a letter collection, but by the nature of his materials and the manner of their use. Of them he made a work which is, as a work of art must be, a magnificent whole. It is, so to speak, a cosmic pageant or drama, in which a gigantesque sequence of meaningful pictures is thrown before the eyes of its readers (or hearers), with the result that they are influenced to do what it is the object of the work to have them do. This is, of course, to nerve them to refuse to participate in the cult of the Emperor, and to inspire them to persist in their refusal.

The messages of Revelation are all with reference to this situation. Taken as such it is a remarkable book. It stands in the whole development of apocalyptic as the last apoc-

alypse properly so-called to be written by a Christian leader.[17]
From this time, in the history of Christian literature, apocalyptic writing wanes. There is, to be sure, a document
which is called the *Apocalypse of Peter,* but it is in no particular typical of the apocalyptic form. It is a thoroughly Greek
work, as is indubitably shown by its conception of punishment after death. Nor is the *Shepherd* of Hermas a true
apocalypse, although it is classified as such by ancient and
modern historians of literature. It is apocalyptic only as it
uses revelation as its epistemological method. It is the
Revelation of John which is the last Christian, as 4 Ezra is
the last Jewish, apocalypse.

The discontinuance of the apocalypse in Judaism and
Christianity was due to different causes. In the latter case
the reason unquestionably was the integration of Christianity
into Graeco-Roman life. Christianity became at home in this
world, so that the basic assumptions of apocalyptic were nega-
tived. Certain of these, or at least certain implications, persisted: Tertullian could repudiate the world and deny the
possibility that the Emperor might be a Christian, but Christianity's progressive integration in this world continued.

In fine, as was seen in the evolution of the gospel materials,
so here, the same forces creating the religious attitudes of the
early Christians are to be observed. Their movement was in
competition with other religious movements — in this case
with the cult of the Emperor — and from conflict it was effecting its own solidarity. The suppression of Christians under Domitian's provincial administrators was a potent force
in precipitating and crystallizing tendencies, attitudes and
teachings among the early Christians.

It is not in place to indicate here the steps by which the

issues took shape and the conflicts worked out. If it is a correct judgment that the stress of suppression is reflected in Josephus' *Antiquities,* in Luke-Acts, Hebrews, Revelation and 1 Clement, the sequence may have been in that order. Josephus sees the distress impending. So does Luke-Acts; it seems to have been the occasion of this work to present the story of Jesus and of the expansion of Christianity defensively in view of the impending crisis.[18] Hebrews reflects an early stage, reminding its readers that they have not found it necessary to resist to the point of bloodshed. But in Revelation the blood is plentiful. One " martyr " can be named; significantly, " Antipas my martyr " is of the Pergameme church, and Pergamum was the seat of the provincial cult of the Emperor. But more blood will be shed at once; Revelation reflects the bloody suppression in progress. First Clement, however, views it from a perspective. It is past, and after it the metropolitan church quietly and firmly asserts itself just as Hebrews had challenged it to do.

As is well known of later situations, persecution, much as it was dreaded and terrible as were its consequences, purged and purified churches; they emerged from it stronger than they had been before. Probably it was so in this earlier instance, particularly since pressure was limited in place and not extensive in time.

But the Christian movement met the Domitianic suppression because it developed the necessary strength. It was represented by numerous well-established churches. Their adherents had developed characteristic attitudes and had achieved distinctive ways of life. That these were now articulated in gospels proves that they were objective and tangible codes. The use of non-gospel writings proves that the religious leaders were versatile. Christianity was rapidly articulating an abundant tradition. It was but natural that some of its leaders reacted favorably and others reacted negatively to innovations, such as written gospels were; it was inevitable that some should prefer old and tried methods and forms. Thus the letters of Paul could be made into an institution. Thus another apocalypse could be written. Thus a homily could be written and circulated — a practice utilized later.

But the innovation which resulted in the writing of gospels actually tended to conserve, for even though the oral transmission of stories of Jesus persisted, even though it may be seen as late as Papias' plain statement of preference for it, the conditions of Christianity's expansion in these days when it was maturing were better served by these objective and tangible forms of the teaching of Jesus than by the orally perpetuated gospel pericopes. The cults of Jesus were now a general Church. The movement which they totalized could properly be called Christianity. The Christianity of the end of the gospel-making period was emerging from its adolescence and steadily moving to its maturity.

PART THREE

AFTER THE GOSPELS

VIII

A PICTURE OF POPULAR CHRISTIANITY

In New Testament study, as any adequate inspection shows, the sources which were written after the gospels have received much less attention than those written earlier.[1] Doubtless this is due to the greater attractiveness of genetic processes, which are necessarily reflected in earlier sources. But the reason is partly, at least, that the later Christian writings are held in lower esteem.

It is true, of course, that Christianity, as is the case with every social movement, passed from an initial stage of creativity to a more prosaic phase of growth. It is true that the later sources, products of the more prosaic period, lack many of the features of charm which characterize the earlier. Nevertheless, since they reflect some of the most important developments in the growth of Christianity, they are of the highest value. Their neglect is regrettable.

For it must be appreciated that situations no less perplexing, no less difficult, no less important faced the Christians after the turn of the first century. Some of them were met in ways which make it valuable to interrogate the later sources which reflect them. That these works are not so charming nor so effective in the esteem of modern Christians ought not to result in their neglect.

Just why the growth of Christianity in the first half of the second century is less interesting, or why the crises which were met and surmounted are regarded as less significant, is not clear. It was during these decades that Christianity became fully conscious of itself, when its solidarity was thoroughly achieved, when its awareness of the meaning of its spread throughout the Roman world was fully appreciated, when it made its decisions as to what forms of internal administration to adopt, when the perception of " the catholic church " was effected, and when it became able to determine that a minority movement within itself was schismatic and heretical — when Christianity became able to measure itself. It was during these years that more than one conflict with the State was met and survived. This was when Christianity made its first bid for acceptance by contemporary cultures, and was thus impelled to state its own point of view in defense with reference to contemporary cultures, religion and political entities. By the time the latest book of the New Testament was written there was hardly an aspect of Christianity's claim upon the ancient world which had not been advanced and the response assured. These were the times when the implications of many of Christianity's internal changes were perceived and accepted. In short, these were the years when Christianity was not merely adventitiously spreading in the Graeco-Roman world, but was consciously planning her course on the basis of deliberate choice. Surely these are processes the knowledge of which should be eagerly sought and highly valued.

It is fitting that this task should begin with the study of a picture of popular Christianity. Especially is this true for the student who desires to learn the characteristics of the religious life which the early Christians actually lived. It is curious and unfortunate, however, that so revealing a source for the study of popular Christianity as the *Shepherd* of Hermas has not received the attention which it deserves. To be sure, this is partially true because the work is extraordinarily prolix, and in large part tedious as well. But the major reason that it is neglected is that few have troubled to understand it, while the few who have made the effort have usually treated it as in a class by itself merely because it is not in the New Testament.

It is true, too, that Hermas presents many difficulties. For one thing, its contents deny the characterization given it in tradition. There is a reference to it in the Muratorian fragment, which remarks that it was written "recently, in our own time, while Pius, the author's brother, occupied the bishop's chair," and that while it may be useful for private reading it must not be read in church. Hermas is classified by the fragment with the apocalypses. It has therefore been studied primarily with reference to the history of the Canon of Christian writings, rather than for its own sake.

When it is studied at all it is found to be composite. This apparent fact, when confronted with the statement of the Muratorian fragment, confuses the student. What was the period of the writing of Hermas? What was the period of the career of the prophet? While there are persuasive facts which point to a relatively earlier date,[2] the contradictory statement of the fragment is usually sufficient to incline judgment toward a later time, so that the task of discovering a sequence of the parts of which the *Shepherd* is composed [3] is likely to seem forbidding.

But when Hermas is regarded as a source of knowledge of popular Christianity, reflecting several stages of evolution in its several parts, and when it is approached to discover its evidence for the religious life of its people, Hermas is found to be an absorbingly interesting work.

The popular level which it reflects, and the interest which it possesses, may at once be seen by reading a bit of its narrative. When this is done on the basis of its Greek text these essential features are apparent.[4] Indeed, they may be suggested by translating a portion in such a manner as approximates its style:

> The man who brought me up sold me to a certain Rhoda in Rome. After many years I realized things and I began to love her like a Christian sister.
>
> Then after a while I saw her bathing in the river Tiber, and I reached out my hand and drew her out of the river. Looking at her beauty I thought to myself, " How happy I would be if I had such a wife, a woman of such beauty and of such a way." This was my only thought — nothing else.
>
> Some time after this, while I was going to Cumae, I was praising God's creation, how great and glorious and mighty it is, as I was walking I fell asleep. And a spirit took me and carried me through an unknown place, through which no man was able to make his way, for the place was rough and cut up by streams. Well, I crossed that river and came to a smooth place, and I got down on my knees and I began to pray to the Lord and to confess my sins. While I was praying the sky was opened, and I see that woman whom I desired greeting me from heaven. She said, " Hello! Hermas! " When I saw her I says to her, " Lady, what are you doing here? " She answered me, " I went up to accuse you to the Lord because of your sins." I says to her, " Are you accusing me right now? " " No," she said, " but listen to the things I am going to say. . . ."

Indeed, so popular and racy is the narrative of Hermas that some critics[5] have thought that the work was made up (among other things) of popular erotic tales which were to a degree " spiritualized." However this may have been, the student quickly sees that the content of Hermas, no less than the style, illustrates the very popular level of Christianity.

This point becomes apparent, even though it has been obscured by scholarly study. Theological interests have controlled much of the previous work on Hermas. For example, one is assured that Hermas was written to exploit a teaching about sin after baptism.[6] This is, indeed, one of the questions to which the work addresses itself, but, as will be shown, the problem is dealt with as a practical disciplinary matter, not theologically nor abstractly. Hermas is eminently practical. Its teaching,[7] of great importance in its general plan, is consistently presented with practical aim.

It is an arresting thought which comes as one reflects that the same Christian group in Rome had among its leaders the well-mannered Clement and the untaught but vigorous Hermas. One is then forced to realize that Christianity in a given locality had a place for the institutionally minded leader who used formal literary method and for the prophet who obtained his guidance and his messages from visions. Moral earnestness is to be found in the urbane ecclesiastic and the crude visionary. It is important that such distinctive types of leadership are to be found at work in these sources. Obviously a following was obtained by the leader representing each type.

Thus the *Shepherd* of Hermas proves that formulations of Christian ways of life were not made by ecclesiastics and theologians alone, but, on the other hand, that they were in some part determined by popular leaders like Hermas. For it was the purpose of Hermas' work to do what other Christian writings have been found to do: to articulate and give direction to proper ways of life.

As has been shown, Hermas' method differed. He was a rude, untaught man. He had been a slave. After obtaining his freedom in some way which is not related, Hermas became a successful business man in a small way. He married, and had a family. Becoming a Christian, he found himself to be one of those to whom vision experiences were vouchsafed. And when he conceived it to be his duty to relate these vision experiences to his fellow Christians in church, he found himself, untaught as he was, to be one of the church's leaders and teachers. He found that he could induce the vision experience by fasting, but the ascetic rigorism which he practiced proved to be deleterious to his health, so that the practice had to be curbed. Finally, he was led to believe it to be his duty to write the story of his experiences, and with them to chronicle the teachings which had been revealed to him. The result is the *Shepherd* of Hermas.

The *Shepherd* is a unique book. It is very different from the well-written 1 Clement. While it is commonly called an apocalypse, it is more different from than similar to a typical apocalypse, such as the Revelation of John or 4 Ezra.

The divisions of the *Shepherd* suggest its nature. It is in three parts. The first is called the Visions. There are nominally five visions, but the fifth is really not a vision as are the others; it is a revelation experience which introduces the second part of the work, the Mandates. These are, as the term implies, the normative materials of the book. There are twelve of them. Then comes the third section, called the Similitudes, which are actually ten extended parables. This section, also, is dominantly didactic.

It is interesting to note that the four visions bring into the story no less than four agents of the visionary messages, while the fifth introduces the Shepherd who remains as the sole mediator of the teachings of the remainder of the book. Of the four it is especially notable that the Church is one. It is a well-established institution, with definite didactic and disciplinary functions. On the other hand, it is noteworthy that Jesus never appears as one of the revealers nor in any way to disseminate instruction.

The subject matter of the prophet's lessons is not difficult to observe, even though Hermas is so long and rambling that the modern reader is likely to become too impatient to master its contents. Practical matters are treated, such as the proper behavior of the church member during persecution, and — this is a constantly recurring theme — the corrupting effects upon one's life of business connections, and, indeed, the entire range of contacts with non-Christians. In other words, the lessons are with reference to the necessity of the Christians living in a world in which by the nature of the case they cannot consider themselves permanently and completely at home. Hermas is much perplexed because the economic ties have a bad effect upon one's religion. Economic relations lead one to offer too many hostages to "the world." It was too probable that when trouble came the economic necessities determined one's course; one maintained the connections required by business, and sacrificed those entailed by his religious life. Indeed, the ordinary friendships of common life had a similar effect; they were usually stronger and more influential than the relations of the religious person to members of his group. Hermas writes to make these things different.

To be sure, Hermas' lessons are quite naïve. For example, his solution of the problem of the ill effect of one's business ties is that the man must see to it that he has only one small business, rather than the manifold affairs which involve far-reaching ramifications. Nor does Hermas actually solve the problem how the Christian is to be in the world and yet not of it; the Similitude which deals with the problem of one's relation to civil law in the light of his responsibility to God's law (Sim. 1) exhibits an acute perception of the problem, but it does not finally deal with it. Perhaps this indicates that Hermas' intellectual ability was too meager to make it possible for him to solve difficult problems. But it is none the less true that he was as successful as not a few other leaders of greater acumen. If his answers only temporarily released the tension of these pressing problems they at least assisted in carrying the Christian community to the point that its numbers enabled it to survive until presently the intellectually distinguished leaders could appear.

It is noteworthy that Hermas conceived the project of disseminating his messages throughout the world. The means was the familiar one of writing them. One of the Visions (ii:4:3) tells that he was directed to provide Clement (the Clement who wrote the Roman church's letter to Corinth?) with a copy which he was to send to foreign cities. Another copy, supplied to a woman named Grapte, presumably a local deaconess, was to be read by her to the widows and orphans, and Hermas was to read a copy himself to the assembly of elders who were in charge of the church.

These plans strikingly suggest how widespread was the idea that leaders had a concern with the welfare of the whole Church, not merely their local church, but with the Church widely distributed. They also show that there was a place, as late as the times when the parts of the *Shepherd* were written, for the rude and untaught prophet to instruct the

Church, as well as a place for the more formally instructed institutional leader. The making up of the whole content of Christian teaching was effected by leaders who operated on the low and popular level, as well as by those whose status was certified, whose efforts were directed to the level of those of whom more might be expected than of simple persons like Hermas.

It is useful to point out that Hermas proceeded, as had certain of his contemporaries and predecessors, in independence of the gospel tradition. When one reads the *Shepherd* to observe what gospels or other writings are reflected in it, the result is scanty indeed. This is not because Hermas was ignorant of the gospel tradition or of the gospels. If he lived in Rome not earlier than the closing years of the first century and during the early years of Trajan, he heard many items of gospel tradition told and retold, and heard at least one gospel (presumably the Marcan) read in church. His contemporary, Clement, also a Roman, exhibits knowledge of the gospel pericopes,[8] Luke-Acts, Hebrews and the Pauline corpus. Doubtless Hermas knew something of all these. But Hermas was a prophet, and, as in the days of Paul, the prophet had other and (as he thought) better means of learning than the reading of documents. The gospels, as was shown, owe their production and preservation to other trends than that represented by the prophet. Prophets like Hermas were not congenially disposed toward literary Christianity. It is no contradiction to this that Hermas wrote his book, for, although he became an author, in this as well as in his capacity as a speaking prophet he represented popular, not literary, Christianity.

The popular quality of the *Shepherd* is to be seen in the

use made of it. One envisages with amusement the reactions of the elders who were the first hearers of the work. Was his brother, Pius, the occupant of the bishop's chair, one of them? Very likely they were bound to admit the validity of his right to declare what had been revealed to him. But doubtless they were of the same mind as the writer of the Muratorian document, who declared that while Hermas might be privately read it was not to be read in church.

It doubtless seems strange to the modern student that the crude visionary, the prophet Hermas, could achieve a place of leadership in his time and place. To one used to a Christian Scripture which, though only in small part, contains elegant rhetoric, to one whose impression of Roman Christianity at the end of the first century is obtained from the Greek of 1 Clement, it may appear that Hermas marks a retrograde stage. Nothing could be farther from the truth. The student must realize that there were always and in all places such leaders as Hermas. One must adjust his conception of early Christianity to fit this fact. He must not conclude that because Hermas did not reach the level of Hebrews, 1 Clement, or James it is to their credit and to his discredit. Their Christianity happens to be more numerously represented, and, being literary, to be more widely read. One should discover the actual quality of the Revelation of John to find an analogy for Hermas on the unliterary side. Hermas does not represent a rarity in early Christian growth; even in later times there were many like him. Note the implication of the statements of the Didache:

Whoever comes to teach you . . . receive him. But if the teacher himself is turned about and teaches another teaching to destroy these things, do not listen to him, but if his teaching is for the increase of

righteousness and knowledge of the Lord, receive him as the Lord.
. . . Do not test nor examine any prophet who is speaking by inspiration . . . but not everyone who speaks by inspiration is a prophet,
unless he has the Lord's way of doing. From his way of doing, then,
the false prophet and the [true] prophet shall be known. And no
prophet who orders a meal while inspired shall eat of it; otherwise
he is a false prophet. And every prophet who teaches the truth, if
he fails to do what he teaches, is a false prophet. But no prophet who
has been tested and is true, doing a cosmic mystery of the church, if
he does not teach others to do what he does himself, shall be judged
by you. . . . But if someone says by inspiration " Give me some
money," or, " Give me something [else]," you must not listen to him;
but if he tells you to give it on behalf of others in need, let no one
judge him.

Obviously this homely advice on a practical subject indicates
the presence of no few in the churches who were more or
less like Hermas; at all events there were many who, like
him, represented uninstructed and popular Christianity.[9]

Probably it was because the others were merely vocal, and
did not, like Hermas, receive the direction to write their
messages, that they are less well known than he. It was the
literate leader who should be regarded as remarkable and
unusual. Of course Christianity came to have persons of
higher attainment than Hermas in its membership. But it
never ceased to have people of his level, and such people,
then as now, made up the great proportion of the membership of the churches.

IX

" BE READY TO SUFFER AS A CHRISTIAN "

The pseudonymous and improperly so-called First Epistle of Peter is largely concerned with the behavior of its people in a situation of persecution. It is perhaps well to remark that by most students of the history of Christian literature it is associated with the traditional persecution of Domitian.[1] The attempt will be made to show, however, that this work, not belonging to the epistolary category, not written by Peter, and functioning in another than the Domitianic situation, has a specific message and an important contribution to make as it is considered as the work of a Christian leader who had his independent solution of a critical problem.

The persecution *motif* is the clew to the understanding of the work. It plunges into this theme: those addressed are urged to rejoice even though they have suffered in many trials. Its practical purpose is with reference to this theme: those addressed are exhorted that if they are called before a court they shall be guilty only of being Christians. This datum is of prime importance. It indicates a fundamental difference between this and earlier situations in the matter of the legal basis of persecution.[2] Until now, so far as can be determined from the sources, no member of the cults of Jesus was persecuted on the ground that he was a Christian. What truth there may be in the tradition that Nero " persecuted "

Christians seems to be that a number were tortured and put to death because they were accused of the burning of Rome, not because they were accused of being Christians. The troubles which came during the time of Domitian arose because of the vigor of the cult of the Emperor at that time; those "persecuted" were harassed because they would not worship the Emperor; that was the decisive point, not merely that they were Christians. Now it is different; one may suffer on the ground that he is a Christian. Being a Christian is a recognized crime.

This datum balances with a well-known situation: that disclosed by the Pliny-Trajan correspondence.[3] The younger Pliny, as governor of Bithynia, wrote to the Emperor to inquire what was the proper procedure in the legal process against Christians. He submitted with his question a statement of what he had been doing. When persons were accused of being Christians, as several had been (some by an anonymous declaration), he caused them to be arrested and examined them. When any denied that they were Christians, and performed such religious acts as proved that they were not (e.g., worshiped the Emperor's image, performed approved sacrifice, or reviled Christ) they were immediately set free. Some admitted that they had been Christians, but had abandoned Christianity, in some cases several years before. Such as confessed that they were Christians were remanded for further examination and perhaps punishment. They were given further opportunity to deny, and pressure, such as the threat of punishment, was brought to bear to encourage denial. If they persisted in confessing in the face of reiterated warning, they were imprisoned in the judgment that if for no other reason their obstinacy merited punishment. To secure information Pliny caused the arrest of two young women (the language makes it difficult to determine whether they were " deaconnesses " or merely women slaves) and put them to torture (it should be remembered that this was neither illegal nor by ancient custom inhuman; it was a legalized manner of obtaining evidence). What he found quite reassured him. Christianity at worst was nothing more than a superstition; its devotees did nothing more serious than meet early in the morning for a love feast in which they took oath to commit no crime during the day, and disperse after singing a hymn. Indeed, Pliny thinks, the spread of Christianity has been checked. For a time it had made marked inroads, spreading from cities to rural districts, with sufficient effect that the sale of produce for temple ritual had seriously fallen off. Now, however, the temples were again being frequented, and the influence of Christianity was notably less.

In his reply Trajan in the main confirmed Pliny's procedure, merely stipulating that no attention be given anonymous accusations. It is important, however, that Trajan plainly indicates that according to law being a Christian was a crime for which the one guilty was liable to punishment. It will be recalled that Ignatius of Antioch is believed to have been put to death in this " persecution." [4]

The essential agreement of the data of 1 Peter and those of the Pliny-Trajan correspondence is remarkable. It strongly argues for the dating of 1 Peter in the traditional Trajanic persecution.

First Peter has further data. It recommends an attitude toward the Emperor which is important in connection with the developments just discussed. This was, indeed, a delicate point. As Paul recommended, members of the cults were expected to be subject to laws and to accept their subjection to administrators. But 1 Peter adds that all men are to be held in honor, the brothers are to be loved, God is to be feared, and the Emperor is to be honored. This is a nice distinction. It has a classic illustration in the *Acts of the Scillitan Martyrs,*[5] who say plainly to their trial-judge: "We render honor to the Emperor as Emperor, but we reverence only God as God." Evidently the ability to make the distinction, as well as the necessity of making it, obtained when 1 Peter was written. It will be observed, too, that the reiterated appeal of 1 Peter is that its public must order their lives so that they shall be liable to punishment for no other reason than that they are Christians, and they are further exhorted that as this question arises they may be able and willing to confess that loyalty.

The persecution data furnish information of the situation and the occasion of the source. Equally interesting and important are those data which exhibit 1 Peter's conception of religion. The writer sees Christianity as essentially simple. The people addressed have been pagans, whose lives have been lived on the patterns common to pagan life. They have come into a cult of Jesus. They are now expected to live differently, in accordance with a new standard and a different morality. They are to become a new people, with lives characterized by a loyalty to the Lord whom they love, although they have never seen him. The emphasis upon the moral life is, as has been pointed out, chiefly with reference to the practical issue presented by persecution. But beyond this it can be seen that the problem is complicated because the cult, as part of the whole movement, is at a point where the distinction of itself from other religious societies and movements must be made. The church is emerging from the nebulous and undefined " spirituality " which was natural in earlier situations. The intellectuality of 1 Peter is slight and of little consequence: the members of the cult have joined it by faith (i.e., belief), but what they believed (and are now expected to believe) was simple. There is not much theology in 1 Peter, perhaps because its author was not interested in this aspect of Christianity, perhaps because he faced problems which at the moment were of greater practical importance.

In brief, 1 Peter reads very much like a plain and earnest appeal to preserve the essential simplicities which had characterized Christianity in its earlier situations as well as in this. This leads to the observation that the religion which its author inculcates is very much like the Pauline type in which the abandonment of earlier religious loyalties in favor of the new is made by simple affirmation of faith (i.e., belief) in the cult Lord, Jesus. In Paul and in 1 Peter the cult Lord is presented as other mysteries present their divine lords.

If it be true that 1 Peter is an attempt to preserve the simplicities of a religion which is similar to the Pauline religion, it may be suggested that it is significant that the present literary method is used, rather than the recently developed gospel form. It is likely that this is not accidental, but is due to the very fact that the old simplicities are affirmed.

What is the literary form of 1 Peter? The apparent epistolary guise, in the light of one's study of the " Epistle " to the Hebrews, will not mislead students. First Peter is epistolary only in having a quasi-epistolary address and conclusion. It is significant that both the address and the conclusion are readily detachable. When attention is centered upon the body of the work, it is important to observe that it reads like an address. Two brilliant suggestions have been made in this connection. One is that the body of 1 Peter may be considered as an address to initiates into a mystery cult.[6] The other, so similar to this that it involves merely the use of Christian for pagan terms, is that it is a bishop's address to a group of candidates for baptism.[7] Inasmuch as the Christian color of 1 Peter is essential, not extraneous, the former suggestion may be merged with the latter; 1 Peter is an address to initiates into a cult, but these are better to be regarded as catechumens than as *mystae*. When 1 Peter is read with this hypothesis in mind, the details so fittingly relate to this suggested purpose, leading up, as they do, to the explicit mention of baptism, that the suggestion becomes irresistible.

The emphasis upon persecution, so far from being out of keeping with this judgment, is entirely relevant to it. It was one thing for those on the fringe of the cult to yield to the pressure of general public opinion, and to reaffirm loyalty to a religious cult approved by the State; it was quite another thing for one who had identified himself as a member of the cult of Jesus, who had received instruction into its mystery, and who had undertaken the full obligation of its initiatory sacrament and was now in full membership, with the responsibilities which that entailed. It must be remembered that this involved the further obligation taken in the cult oaths of the *agape*.

The attachment of an epistolary conclusion is not incongruous. If, as this hypothesis assumes, 1 Peter is a bishop's address to candidates for baptism such a means of securing circulation of the message throughout the " diocese " would be effective and therefore natural. The problem of address, however, is more difficult. It is bound up with the larger question of pseudonymity: why was this work circulated under Peter's name? It is hardly necessary to argue that Peter did not write it; the excellence of the Greek might, as has been repeatedly said, have been contributed by an amanuensis, but the typically Pauline type of the religious life reflected is hardly consonant with Peter's authorship. Neither is the obvious literary relation with the collection of Pauline letters, not to mention the use of the same *Haustafel* as that used by Paul. These phenomena put the matter beyond doubt. First Peter is a pseudonym, but how and why was this particular literary convention used?

The hypothesis which seems to have the highest credibility is that in 1 Peter the Roman church is again speaking, this time in the name of one of the two great leaders which it claimed as its founders. Stirred to active and aggressive leadership by the challenge of " Hebrews," it not only met the Domitianic persecution, but it maintained its position of leadership when another, this time a more clearly defined, issue arose. The provinces listed in the address may be understood simply as suggesting that the matters treated in the " letter " are intended for general cognizance.

It is hoped that the foregoing discussion has maintained a proper distinction between inference and conjecture. Such a distinction needs to be drawn. Thus Canon Streeter's suggestion that the author of 1 Peter was Aristion belongs merely to the category of conjecture. It is always attractive to be able, if only in imagination, to attach a document to a particular person, and it is interesting that what is known of Aristion suits Streeter's suggestion. However, the greater effectiveness of the document when it is viewed as the message of the Roman church is not only a major reason for maintaining the judgment offered above, but the further coincidence of the Pliny-Trajan correspondence gives added force.

So viewed, 1 Peter is an illuminating source of information for the study of early second century Christianity. The movement is seen in greater vigor, as befits its longer experience. It is seen in new aspects, as befits its otherwise well-attested variety. It is thus natural that it is in working independence of the gospel tradition, for the written gospels did not dominate the early churches as they dominate the modern. That plain and simple leaders were able to meet new situations shows that the Christian movement had not lost its vitality; that some met new situations by maintaining older types of experience is witness of that independence of gospel tradition which has been noted.

It is the interplay of the old and the new in 1 Peter which fixes this work in the achievement of particular character in early Christianity. As has been said, the basic and fundamental elements in the religious life which it reflects come, as was true of the Pauline groups, upon belief in Jesus, confession, and baptism into the cult. It should be observed with due emphasis that 1 Peter 4:7-11 maintains in detail a number of the values characteristic of Pauline Christianity, including an emphasis upon the charismata (indeed, using the very term). And the writer of 1 Peter finds it in keeping with his way of inculcating moral instruction to cite, in somewhat extended form, the table of household duties first encountered in Colossians. But it should not be supposed that the religious life reflected in 1 Peter has no new features. Doubtless it is because the work makes an advance upon Pauline religious experience that its use of mystery cult terminology is more obvious in its detail and inclusiveness. It is a distinctively new feature, however — and one in particular independence of gospel tradition — that the *decensus* item, having come into the general tradition, is used by the writer of 1 Peter. It is noteworthy, to allude to a matter of behavior rather than of teaching, that the new elements in the table of household duties show that Christians are meeting new questions of custom: it appears to be necessary for the writer of 1 Peter to warn against adopting non-Christian manners of dress, wearing of jewelry and coiffure; it may also be inferred that slaves are sometimes restless and need to be warned to be always respectful.

Even more indicative of new feature is that which appears when the emphasis upon the distinction between the old life and the new life is observed. The people of the cult used to live with pagans as pagans, but now they live differently, and their former associates are surprised and offended that they have withdrawn from their former associations. Indeed, the fact is basic to the troubles which the cult members face, for their old companions now abuse them because they have withdrawn and live differently. Another feature of distinction marks a similar advance over the primitive status: these people are now conscious of distinction from Jews. They are at the threshold, if, indeed, they have not stepped over it, of the soon-to-become-usual conception: that the people of the cults of Jesus have supplanted the Jews and are therefore the true Israel. And obviously the emphasis in 1 Peter upon ecclesiastical organization, particularly in the matter of the cult practices, is a further growth from the essentially simple base. The Christians, for they may now be called that without committing an anachronism, have already appropriated a number of figures from Jewish Scripture to justify this; they are the chosen race, a royal priesthood, a consecrated nation, God's people.

The writer of 1 Peter proceeds as he recommends. Very likely he practiced charismatic inspiration, which may well have been a reason why, although he writes when many gospels were in existence, he quotes none. When he quotes it is Jewish Scripture, always for its evidential value and in an apologetic manner. His direct teaching is, indeed, the result of his possession of a charism, for when he speaks he does it as one who utters the oracles of God (4:11).

Thus in its reaffirmation of earlier conceptions and values, no less than in its adoption and advancement of newer features, 1 Peter bears witness to transformations taking place in Christianity. It was in the variety of types of experience, variety of leadership, and particularly in the differing exigencies of situations that necessary adaptations were made and further changes effected.

X

THE TEACHER EXPOUNDS HIS CODE

The homily and the apocalypse written by Christian leaders while others were writing gospels show that a variety in the types of religious experience in early Christianity produced different types of religious leadership. These differences are reflected in the several forms of the literary vehicles of religious teaching.

The student will discover that the didactic function in Christianity was itself expressed in various ways. There were teachers in the Pauline communities, and while it is not known in detail what their work was it is certain that it was of the non-gospel type. The didactic function was one important element, among others, in articulating the gospel traditions, but it was only one of several aspects of the leadership which produced the gospels from the gospel materials and sources.

Not long after the gospels were written two different types of Christian writing appeared which exhibit the work of the specialized teacher. Both are of other than the gospel form. One of them is called " The Teaching of the Lord Jesus through his Twelve Apostles," commonly called *The Didache,* and the other is the so-called Epistle of James. Both are interesting in their own right, and both are instructive when they are compared with the gospels.

Modern gospel study directs attention especially to what is

called, in view of contemporary emphasis upon form, the paraenetic materials of the gospels. These are, as the term indicates, elements of teaching which by exhortation undertake to influence persons to live according to generalized norms in patterns which apply to all situations, rather than to one specific situation. Christian paraenesis arose through contacts of early Christians with their environments, recognizing local patterns and adapting them to Christian use. The table of household duties, found in a Pauline letter and subsequently used widely, is a case in point. Certain parts of the gospels present other examples and reflect other stages in the processes of the growth of paraenesis. Additional information is furnished by the work of teachers in the post-gospel period.

The *Didache* is especially instructive. Like the gospels, it owes its final form to the incorporation of sources.[1] Again, it illustrates in some of its content the continued existence of gospel materials as separate pericopes. Further, it contains a considerable amount of independent material. Much more obviously than in the gospels the church appears as fully developed, institutionalized, and manned by officials; its " services " of several types are their specialized field of activity. What is especially illuminating, as is also true of the Epistle of James, is its concern for the definition of the moral code of the church member. In this respect the *Didache* is a particularly valuable example of early Christian paraenesis.

Doubtless the most interesting feature of the *Didache,* to modern readers, is its approximation of the content of the gospel traditions. Does it quote the gospels? Certainly some of its materials are introduced directly, without the guise of quotation. Others are introduced as " the teaching of the words (*logia*)," some as " commandments." On the other hand, the gospel is sometimes referred to as meaning generally "the good news." Once the words occur, " the ordinance (*dogma*) of the gospel," but the item so introduced has no parallel in any known gospel. Another teaching is cited with the sanction, " as you find in the gospel," although no identifiable reference can be determined. Once " the gospel of our Lord " is referred to in a general way which suggests a specific reference; the so-called Lord's Prayer is cited essentially as it appears in the gospel according to Matthew (significantly, in the form with the doxology) with the formula, " as the Lord commanded in his gospel." A quotation which corresponds closely with another saying in Matthew has the formula " concerning this the Lord said." In spite of the apparently direct quotation of Matthew it is uncertain whether this work is actually quoted, or whether " the gospel " has more general meaning. Certainly materials are included which were not derived from any gospel known to us, and, indeed, the whole of the *Didache* is affirmed as independent teaching.

It must be remembered that inspired teaching is assumed by the *Didache* as being still in use (11:3-12, quoted above, p. 142f.). And the differences from the known gospels are as noteworthy as the apparent relations with any one.

The *Didache,* while it is instructive to study it together with James, is not similar to the " Epistle " of James at every point. Each in its own way is a valuable source for the study of the work of the teacher expounding his code. The ecclesiasticism of the *Didache* has only slight representation in James, and the *Didache* much more obviously refers its teaching to source. There are several interests in the *Didache* not present in James, e.g., the careful instruction about holding the sacraments (interestingly enough, in these aspects the teaching differs markedly from that of the gospels), and the criteria for qualifying church officials. It is a further interesting detail that the *Didache,* put into its present shape at some time during the second century, includes with teaching of the Lord a thoroughly apocalyptic section.

But James and the *Didache* are similar in that both exhibit a teacher who has here articulated and is here expounding a code of moral standards for Christian people. Indeed, the work of the teacher is specifically referred to (Did. 11:1, 2, 10–12; James 3:1). That the more apparent correspondences with the gospel traditions are fewer in James (cf. 3:12, 4:10, 5:12), and that its teachings are introduced quite independently, without formula of any sort, does not invalidate the characterization just made. Quotations of Scripture are few (2:8, 11, 23, 4:6) and allusions fewer (4:5, 5:11, 17). This does not indicate that the writer of James did not know Scripture; although Septuagint quotations are few the terminology of the Greek Old Testament is abundantly reflected throughout its vocabulary.[2] The point is that James does not proceed on the basis of Scripture quotation or allusion; it is itself an independent piece of teaching, which does not utilize such authority for sanction.

The literary form of James is a useful clew to its nature and a useful means for understanding its function. To a remarkable degree James approximates the literary form of the Cynic-Stoic diatribe.[3] In other words, the "Epistle" of James, which is epistolary only in that it has been given a quasi-epistolary salutation, is the work of a leader who has adapted to the purposes of Christian didactic the vehicle which had proved so useful in disseminating the Stoic morality. The Christian used to inculcate in his code the method long since developed by the Stoic teacher. James is to be compared with Hebrews in being an example of spoken rhetoric; it may be called a homily, if it be remembered that the ancient conception of the homily, as distinct from the modern, did not require the development of some one given theme.[4]

It is of the utmost importance to remember that the writer, or, better, the speaker of James is, as was suggested, expounding his code. The moralities of James are generalities.[5] The distinctive feature of James, that which permits its classification as paraenesis, is that its teachings are intended for general, not for specific, reference. The difference between James' paraenesis and the hortatory sections of a Pauline letter is that each example of Paul's practical moralizing was with reference to some specific and individual case, and is not intended to be general in nature, while in the case of James it is impossible, because it was not intended, to find a situation which it was particularly designed to meet. Its persons are types, not individuals; its cases of moral issue are general, not particular. This is the nature of paraenesis. Thus it is in Christian paraenesis that the moral patterns of early Christianity are found. As has been mentioned, the gospels in part exhibit aspects of the growth of paraenesis, while still other aspects are illustrated by such other didactic works as have been cited.

The literature of the Graeco-Roman world further illustrates the processes. Perhaps the most instructive commentary on James is the work known as Pseudo-Phocylides.[6] This Greek poem, a series of aphorisms, has many passages which closely parallel, and many others which in some manner illustrate the teachings of James. For example:

Give to the poor man at once, nor tell him to come on the morrow,
When thy right hand is filled full, share what thou hast with the
    needy.
Not in thy strength make thy boast, nor yet in thy wisdom or riches,
God and none other is strong, and wise and all-blessed in all things.
Render not evil for evil; vengeance commit to the judges.
Use discretion in speech; naught is more choice than discretion;
Thoughtful speech to a man is a weapon sharper than iron.
Heed the first glimpse of an evil; neglect not a sore that seems trifling;
Look from how tiny a spark a forest's expanse can be kindled!
Shun every cause of division, and dread war's murderous clamor.

Many another hexameter of Pseudo-Phocylides might be cited to parallel the didactic of James; these are typical and sufficiently representative.

Clearly James and Pseudo-Phocylides represent the same process. What was it? The attempts at answering this question have led to much darkening of counsel, inasmuch as students of both works have operated upon the basis of presuppositions which inevitably beg the question. It is tacitly assumed by many that the moral genius of the ancient world was peculiarly vested in the Jewish people, so that wherever a piece of ethical teaching is found it is concluded that it must be Jewish. Thus Pseudo-Phocylides is commonly classified as Jewish-Greek literature.[7] Why this should be so is not apparent; there is nothing particularly Jewish about it. It is merely because the work is predominantly moral in purpose, and somewhat comparable in form to the Jewish Wisdom Literature that it is supposed to be Jewish in origin. While it is quite possible that Jewish morality influenced the Graeco-

Roman world, it seems gratuitous to infer by such reasoning that Pseudo-Phocylides is Jewish-Greek.

Indeed, the analogies furnished by Tobit and the Ahikar stories suggest that the primary influence was that of gentile culture affecting Judaism; these works, like Wisdom, represent Hellenistic Judaism in which the basic element is gentile. Nor does the parallel with the Wisdom Literature deserve much consideration; the much closer approximation of the literary form of the diatribe clearly outweighs it. The study of James in the light of Pseudo-Phocylides shows that early Christian teachers were doing much the same as other moral teachers (compare Isocrates, *ad Nicolem,* and Pseudo-Isocrates, *ad demonicum*) were doing. The work of one illustrates the work of another.

The so-called Epistle of James is thus to be viewed as a post-gospel articulation of Christian paraenesis, to some degree similar to (compare 5:12), but independent of, the gospel tradition. In it one sees a teacher who is either unacquainted with the gospels or deliberately ignores them. Evidently he considers the literary form of the diatribe as preferable, and by means of it he sets forth his patterns of Christian idealism.

Naturally, since the teaching of James is essentially general, it is difficult, if not impossible, to determine the time and place in Christianity which it represents. What it is and what it does are clear, but it is not so obvious when and where its work was done. Attempts to determine authorship, date and place are greatly at variance. The basic question, whether the work is a pseudonym, has a generally affirmative answer; James was a common Greek name, so that if the work is a pseudonym its ascription to one James must have been with a certain James in mind. A persistent tradition is that the James intended was the brother of Jesus, later the bishop of Jerusalem in tradition. There is one grave difficulty in entertaining this ascription. The excellence of the Greek must have been obvious to any ancient leader who desired to recommend his teaching by ascribing it to James of Jerusalem; it must have been apparent that this would hardly suit the ascription. And the late achievement of " James " of a place in the canon of Christian writings is fatal to the judgment that James of Jerusalem actually wrote it; Origen was the first to affirm it. In spite of this the alleged similarities to the gospels are thought by some to suggest authorship by this James. However, modern work on the gospels points in the opposite direction: the coincidences between James and the gospels occur because each is an independent articulation of Christianity's teachings. The paraenetic materials of the gospels had a long and a varied history; if they reappear in non-gospel form in such works as James and the *Didache* it is because the teacher in early Christianity fulfilled his task in many ways.

On the whole, it seems to be most satisfactory to regard James as reflecting some undetermined Graeco-Roman locality at a certain point in Christianity's emerging maturity. A date in the second century is required by considerations of canonicity, but it is impossible to be more definite about it. Obviously it was either a non-Pauline locality, or one in which the Pauline type of the religious life had given way to a more prosaic, but withal to a more objective and tangible one.

Primitive problems and characteristics of primitive Christian life do not appear in the work. James is interested in articulating a code, not in discovering the answers to new questions. The problems dealt with are those of a movement which is far from its beginning, i.e., generalized questions of wealth and poverty.[8]

There is a definite ecclesiastical aspect of the religious movement represented by James, as well as by the *Didache*. As has been mentioned, the *Didache* devotes much more space to matters of ritual and institutionalism, but James' reference to church officials concerned with the healing of the sick shows that the church figures in his code as the fundamental means of institutionalizing it. This is much the same as is true of the *Didache*.

The function of the church seals the observation that James is properly to be understood as a source for the study of Christianity's consolidation. The emphasis upon teaching is merely the specialization of the author's work. Characteristically, he proceeds by enunciating normative patterns, using (as was consonant with the diatribe style) as most effective means the rhetorical question and the imperative.[9] He illustrates the Christian movement as coming to terms with its world, so much so that his important contribution to the growth of Christianity is the making of its moral patterns conventional. The details of his code he derived from living experience in Hellenistic life, articulating them in language long since found effective in the phrasing of moral instruction. He expresses his teachings on the basis of his authority as a church official, a recognized teacher. He makes no effort to secure sanction, as the gospels did, by ascribing them to Jesus, but he presents them as the proper function of the Christian teacher.

The student must content himself with the rich store of information derivable from James about the consolidation of Christianity to compensate him for the impossibility of learning more about its author, its date, and its place.

XI

THE RISE OF SECTARIAN PROBLEMS

The presence of a variety of tendencies in Christianity as the movement began to consolidate made it inevitable that problems should be precipitated by the rise of sects and heresies. Unfortunately, almost every study of Christianity which deals with this aspect has approached these problems with a wrong emphasis. The goal has been to identify the sectarian group by determining exactly how its heretical beliefs differed from those of the general movement. This has erroneously suggested that sectarian problems were essentially intellectual, and were so regarded by the early leaders.

As has been emphasized in the present study, the varieties in early Christianity were with reference to ways of living the religious life. The consolidation of Christianity involved the articulation of the codes and patterns, so that early Christian didactic was very largely with reference to behavior. Thus the emergence of sectarian problems was a social, rather than an intellectual, matter. The basic question was that of discipline, rather than belief.

Probably the earliest reflection of a sectarian problem is that which occurs in the little letter which now constitutes the sixteenth chapter of Romans. This source points out that certain persons are causing divisions and scandalous situations which contradict the teaching which Paul had given. The group addressed (was it the Ephesian church?) was advised to take note of these persons and to turn away from them, i.e., to ostracize them. Thus early was discipline of a sort used to meet the problem of division.

Again, the speech to the Ephesian elders (note the Ephesian locale) put into Paul's mouth by the writer of Luke-Acts recognizes as though by anticipation the rise of division which without doubt had arisen when Luke-Acts was written. Grievous wolves were to arise among the Ephesians, while from their own number men were to appear breaking up the unity of the group.

Sectaries are apparent in the situation of the Fourth Gospel (commonly regarded as Ephesian in its provenience). Here the John the Baptist sectaries are all but named. Obviously the sectarian problem is involved in the prayer for unity which climaxes Jesus' discourse for the guidance of the New Community.

Likewise the watchword of unity, no less than the warning against being blown about by every wind of teaching, so important in the messages of " Ephesians," indicates the rise of the sectarian problem.

Finally, it is in his letter to the Ephesian church that the seer of Revelation alludes to the heretical group, the first to be named, called the Nicolaitans.

However, it is in the sources of the post-gospel period that the rise of sects becomes so pressing a problem that its issues now clearly emerge. This is only natural, since Christianity reached its maturity in the period reflected by these works. The movement had first to achieve a consciousness of itself. This had been done; an early stage is reflected in Luke-Acts. Indeed, more had been accomplished: the conception of the church as a general and a geographically widespread institution had been achieved, as " Ephesians " and the Pauline corpus show. First Peter makes plain that people now were liable to suffer as Christians. Then, as will be pointed out presently, a leader of the post-gospel period was able to refer at once to " Christianity " as such and to " the catholic church." And, as has been noted, the Roman church had risen to a dominating position, which could be exercised in practical assertion of control over other churches and in a generalized conception stated in 1 Clement.

The first clear-cut appearance of sectarian problems is found in the Johannine letters. Their writer is a religious leader (doubtless a bishop, since he asserts authority over a district) who attempts to maintain control over his people in the face of a rebellious situation in which some who used to be in the group have left it and are setting up a rival movement. He writes three documents. One of these is plainly a letter addressed to a man named Gaius. A second has an address which because two of its words are ambiguous presents a problem; " the elect Kyria " might be an unnamed woman (" *kyria* " means " lady "), a woman named Kyria, or a figurative address to a church. A third document, much longer than the other two, is commonly called a letter, but it lacks either epistolary salutation or conclusion. It is, however, a document written for more or less general circulation. The problems of the sectaries appear in all three sources. Hence it is an attractive hypothesis that there are by the same leader two letters, one to an individual, another to a church, and a writing which, of other than epistolary form, is a document for the instruction of people generally throughout the leader's sphere of influence, i.e., his diocese.[1]

The problems may be stated most readily by analyzing the sources in that order.

In the third document, a letter so small that it is comparable to the thousands of non-literary papyri, the bishop commends the practice of Gaius in receiving certain traveling members of other societies into fellowship. Also approved is a certain Demetrius. On the other hand, a rebellion is indicated in what is said of Diotrephes, who appears to be a recognized leader in the group in which Gaius also has a position of responsibility; Diotrephes has refused to receive the persons who were hospitably welcomed by Gaius. And, it appears, Diotrephes has also refused to receive the writer of the letter. Further, he has exercised his position of leadership to expel from fellowship the people who have accepted these new arrivals. No reason is given why these people came, why Diotrephes refused to accept them, why he expelled their hosts, or why he thus repudiated the directions stipulated by the letter writer. It will be noted that the writer says that he wrote to the church, only to find that Diotrephes had repudiated his directions.

Two further items are worthy of mention. Not unnaturally, the writer refers to Diotrephes in uncomplimentary terms; he suggests that what standing Diotrephes enjoys he has secured by his own desire for pre-eminence, and implies that what Diotrephes does is wrong and wicked. One of his faults is that he speaks against the writer of the letter; this and his expulsion of the migrants and their hosts are his specific acts of disobedience. The second point is that the writer hopes to clear up the bad situation by writing to Gaius, but he indicates that if necessary he will visit the troubled church, thus implying that if the letter is not sufficient to win its purpose his appearance in person undoubtedly will.

The scant didactic reference in the letter is, in spite of the letter's brevity, surprising. Aside from remarking that the writer rejoiced when some brothers came to him testifying to Gaius' truth, and the general remark that he is never so happy as when he hears of his children walking in truth, there is only the broad exhortation to imitate the good rather than the evil. Obviously these moralizings are to be viewed in the light of the disciplinary crisis. Even so, that no further attempt is made to define basic principles nor to cite relevant teaching is surprising.

The content of the second letter indicates that it was addressed to a church. This is suggested, not merely because " the elect kyria " is probably figurative (Kyria would be less likely, though possible, as a name, and " elect lady," while sufficiently honorific, is hardly cordial enough as addressed to a specific and a well-known person), but because of the several references to the " children." In the final sentence " the children of your elect sister " are referred to, analogously to " your children " who are twice mentioned. The second reference is all but explicit, for in it these " children," who are part of the whole group whose conduct is praised (while that of others is blamed), most probably symbolize the members of a church.

The rebelling persons are mentioned twice, once in a general reference, once in a specific statement. It is said that many deceivers have gone out into the world, persons who are deceivers because they do not confess the belief that Jesus came physically. The members of the church are warned against these deceivers, and are instructed to refuse fellowship to them, even to the point of shutting them from all association — they are not allowed even to greet them. Some, but not all, of the "children" walk in truth, just as "we received commandment from the Father." This clearly indicates the problem of division, as the other letter exploits the disciplinary problem. The solution offered is in exhorting all to obey the commandment which they had from the beginning, i.e., that they love one another. Obviously, in view of the order to refuse hospitality to certain persons, the exhortation to love one another is intended to apply only to the obedient members of the group.

In distinction from the letter to Gaius, this letter introduces general principles and enunciates basic directions. The obedient are persons who are recognized as knowing the truth, and in this matter it is said that the truth is "in us" and that it will remain "with us forever." Therefore the obedient walk in truth. They must continue to obey the old commandment to love one another; indeed, they must walk after God's commandments. Unfortunately, what these commandments are is not stated. On the other hand, the disobedient are characterized in opposite terms. Anyone who takes a position of leadership but does not abide in the teaching of Christ does not possess God. Again, it is unfortunate that this teaching is not specified. Rather, it is merely said that he who abides in the teaching has both the Father and the Son. Presumably the content of the teaching was known to the readers of the letter, for it is further directed that if anyone comes to them without it such persons are to be recognized as those to whom fellowship and hospitality are to be refused. Of course, the approved teaching was the particular orthodoxy of the group in which the writer exercises authority. Indeed, in the degree to which his in-struction is accepted and respected it is the teaching of the group. Perhaps that was why it was unnecessary to specify it.

It is plain that the situation, as far as these two letters re-veal it, was disciplinary and social rather than doctrinal or otherwise intellectual. The attachment of the epithet " anti-christ" to those opposed is merely the usual manner of weak-ening the authority of the rebels by labeling them, especially by applying epithets of obviously opprobrious implication.

In this letter, too, the possibility of a personal visit is men-tioned. Here, however, the tone is entirely friendly, inas-much as the persons addressed acknowledge the writer's authority.

The fuller content of the third document, the " First Epistle of John," complicates the picture. Yet the problems of the rebellion appear at several points. With the many general references to the fellowship, which should be so re-garded, there are explicit statements. One is that " they went out from among us, although they were not of us, for if they had been of us they would have continued with us " (2:19). Hardly less plain is the longer passage discussing the neces-sity of distinguishing " spirits " (4:1ff). The point is simple. Many false prophets have gone out into the world, and the case has arisen in which " spirits " induced by these must be distinguished from the spirit of God. The test is a simple one: the spirit of God is recognized when the inspired person confesses that Jesus appeared physically, whereas any other utterance is *ipso facto* evidence that the spirit is that of antichrist.

Involved in this, of course, is the fact that there is a differ-ence between the " we-group," i.e., the writer and those obedient to him, and the others who are labeled as those of the spirit of error. Finally the entire matter appears in further implications; the group who are commended are they who love God and their fellows, while on the other hand there are those who do not love their fellows, so that it is idle to suppose that they love God.

The distinctions which are indicated by the various slogans or mottoes cited exhibit the same features. Some of the rebels say such things as, " We have fellowship with him," " We have no sin," " I know him," " I abide in him," " I am in the light," " I love God," but from the writer's point of view their behavior contradicts what they affirm.

It is not difficult to reconstruct some of the tenets of the recalcitrant group. The repeated emphasis upon the necessity of acknowledging that Jesus came physically gives the essential clew. The persons who deny it are either the definitely known " seemists " (*docetae*), or persons like them; in either case persons who affirmed that Jesus did not actually suffer because he did not have the physical being necessary for suffering, but that Jesus was a spirit-person whose apparent body was not real and who therefore could not actually experience suffering but merely seemed to do so.

However, it is not desired to center attention upon the opinions of the *docetae* in general nor upon the opinions opposed in these sources.[2] It is essential to have in mind that the situation was primarily social. The all important element in the writer's problem is that the defection of these persons, in the degree to which it was effective and influential, has broken the unity of the whole group. The writer acts to control that situation.

Other elements in the largest source further corroborate

this point of view. For example, certain institutions of the church are involved. The affirmation of the seceders is that they are sinless, i.e., perfectionists. This leads the writer to point out that all are sinners, and that upon occasion anyone may sin, but that in such case we (note the distinction of the " we " implying the " they ") have a Defender with the Father, Jesus Christ the Just, who is the propitiation for our (*sic*) sins and for the sins of the entire world. Again, the manner in which the subsequent argument involves the well-known references to water and blood adds evidence. Obviously the institutions of baptism and the communion are involved. It is to be inferred that only those within the group are eligible to the benefits of these sacraments. Such is the point of the distinction between the witness of God and the witness of men; the sacraments and the third witness, i.e., the spirit, witness God, and the witness of men is in every way inferior.

These, too, are matters which ultimately involve discipline. Obviously the aggressive leader must keep the sacraments and other institutions of the church under his control. One essential point is that the people who receive and benefit by sacraments must accede to their official administration.

It is time to return to the observation that the largest document has a number of interests. The point is suggested by the question of its literary form. It has been remarked that the source lacks epistolary salutation and conclusion. In fact, the opening phrases constitute one of the major problems of the work. They are a curious congeries of relative clauses, with no defining antecedent and unresolved for the lack of a conclusion. Indeed, the opening " verses " as they stand are quite untranslatable. How, for example, should the phrase, "about the word of life," be construed? The best suggestion is the conjecture that it is a scribe's (not, of course, the author's) title for the whole work or for a section of it, the phrase having been inadvertently incorporated.[3]

To be sure, the lack of epistolary equipment is not important; the student of early Christian literature should be accustomed to imperfect approximation of form. The nature of the work may be discovered inductively. When it is analyzed a homiletic source may be identified, which is the basis of the discourse amplified to make the whole document.[4] Thus the "letter" may be viewed as the church leader's (the bishop's) address to a congregation in the celebration of the *agape*,[5] the love feast, amplified by such other matter as the writer considers useful. The whole document is thus the bishop's appeal to his people to submit to his authority. The appeal is the more effective if it was, indeed, based upon the *agape*, for it was essential in this ceremony to take a series of oaths. When "1 John" is re-examined with this hypothesis in mind the suggestion attains some probability. All the elements of the document on this point of view fall into relationship, so that the work thus has fresh meaning.

All three New Testament sources which first reflect the problems precipitated by the rise of sectaries are illuminated when they are studied together with certain contemporary Christian writings. Allusion has been made to the fate of Ignatius of Antioch. Ignatius when on his way as a prisoner to Rome wrote a series of letters,[6] several to Asian churches and one to Polycarp, bishop of Smyrna. So closely do details of the Ignatian letters correspond with elements in the

" Johannine letters " that it is profitable to view them together.

The theme which is common in the Johannine and the
Ignatian letters is that of the unity of the church under the
authority of the bishop. The two sets of writings agree in
conceiving the problem as disciplinary rather than as intellectual. Ignatius insists that the bishop represents the church
in such a manner that no one who is insubordinate to him is
truly within the church, while no one outside the church has
the bread of God. Obviously the reference, like that of
1 John, is to the sacramental meal. The matter is eminently
practical; Ignatius insists that " he who does not come to the
meeting (interestingly enough, the phrase is the same as that
which makes one of the difficult locutions of Luke-Acts, *epi
to auto*) is overbearing and has separated himself (Eph.
5:3)." Throughout the Ignatian letters the data which exhibit the actual appearance of separatism are abundant, e.g.,
Eph. 7:1, 9:1, 20:2; Magnesians 4:1; Trallians 7:2; Philadelphians 3:1–3; 4; Smyrneans 6:2–8. The point reiterated
is that the disavowal of the authority of the bishop breaks up
the unity of the group. Every care must be taken, by bishops
and by people alike, to preserve the corporate unity which
inheres in the loyal relationship of the bishop, the elder, the
deacons and the people.

It is easy to show the social nature of the divisions which
Ignatius deplores. "There are some who recognize the
bishop in their words but who disregard him in their practice.
These . . . do not hold legal meetings according to commandment " (Mag. 4). In a passage strongly suggesting
the words of 1 Clement 48:8 Ignatius says: " Do not attempt
to make anything appear to be right for you according to

your own judgment, but let there be in the assembly one prayer, one petition, one mind, one hope in love . . . come together as it were in one sanctuary of God, as it were to one altar, to one Jesus Christ" (Mag. 7:1, 2). "He who is within the sanctuary is cleansed, but he who is outside the sanctuary is not cleansed, that is, he who is apart from the bishop and the presbytery and the deacons is not cleansed in his conscience" (Trall. 7:2). "As many as are of God and of Jesus Christ, these are with the bishop; as many as change their ways and come to the unity of the church, these, too, shall be of God" (Philad. 3:2). "Be careful, then, to make use of one Eucharist only, for there is one flesh of our Lord Jesus Christ, one cup for union with his blood, one altar, just as there is one bishop with the presbytery and the deacons" (*ibid.* 4).

Ignatius points out the effect of division upon the religious life. Whether objectively or not he alleges (to transliterate the Greek) that the heterodox have no regard for love, none for the widow, for the orphan, for the distressed, for the afflicted, for the imprisoned, or for those released from prison, none for the hungry or thirsty. Further, they absent themselves from the Eucharist and from prayer (Smyr. 6:2–7:1). He recommends that the people be dealt with much as Paul and the writer of 2 John had advised; they are to be noted and avoided, if possible even to be ignored in public or private address.

To be sure, the intellectual aspects of the sectarian problem are not ignored in the Ignatian letters. Like the unnamed bishop, he alludes to their distinctive point of view, i.e., the belief that Jesus merely seemed to suffer (Trall. 10; Smyr. 2, 3, 5). He refers also to heretical inclinations toward Judaism (Mag. 8–10; Philad. 6:1); however, it is less the intellectual, and more the practical element which is here emphasized.

But the practical side of the emphasis upon corporate unity is unmistakable in the view of the bishop of Antioch. He plainly says: "See that you follow the bishop . . . and the presbytery . . . and reverence the deacons. Let no one do any of the things which belong to the church apart from the bishop. Let that be regarded as a legal Eucharist which is held either by the bishop or by one whom he appoints. Wherever the bishop may appear, there let the whole number be present, just as the catholic church is wherever Jesus may be. It is not proper to baptize or to observe an *agape* apart from the bishop, but whatever he may approve, this is pleasing to God, so that everything you do may be legal and certain " (Smyr. 8).

It is plain that to Ignatius, as it was in the case of the other bishop whose diocese was disturbed by disruptive persons, the institutional values in the problem of control were primary. This has been abundantly shown in the matter of the sacraments and the church services. The rise of Scripture to such a status can be seen in an interesting passage: " I entreat you not to practice factiousness, but to live in accordance with Christian teaching. For I heard certain men saying, 'If I do not find it in the archives (*archeiois*) I do not believe in the gospel,' and when I said to them that it was written they answered me, saying, 'That is just the question.' But to me the archives are Jesus Christ, the unchangeable archive is his cross, death, and resurrection, and the faith which is through him " (Philad. 8:2). This passage will be discussed later; here it is relevant to point out that it illustrates how Scripture in Ignatius' conception is but slightly used with reference to didactic interests, except as these are involved in the disciplinary interests.

Similarly, certain elements of the intellectualism of Ignatius actually are effective with reference to disciplinary functions. The most important instance is the manner in which quasi-creedal slogans operate to define a loyalty as well as a faith. Ignatius uses statements of belief in a manner which strongly suggests steps in the growth of the later common creed, but his purpose in so doing is certainly disciplinary (Trall. 9, Smyr. 1).

It is apparent that Ignatius and the writer of the Johannine letters have problems in which many elements were shared. Both thus witness similar developments in Christianity. It is instructive that they attempt to meet their common problems in essentially the same way. To be sure, Ignatius is much more obviously an institutionalist. As compared with his fellow bishop he is much more volatile and emotionally unstable; indeed, there is abundant evidence of psychic abnormality in Ignatius.[7] The New Testament leader is considerably more effective in his use of language; he much more nearly approaches something like the creativity which characterized earlier Christianity. On the other hand, Ignatius merits recognition for the uncompromising consistency with which he asserts his case.

Attention is inevitably drawn to the question of the authorship of the "Johannine letters." This question has deliberately been left to the last, because it is regarded as least important. There is no value whatever in discussing as such "the (five) Johannine writings."[8] If it is not certain that different writers produced Revelation and the Fourth Gospel, nothing in New Testament study is certain. Further, close study assembles grave reasons for concluding that different writers produced the gospel and the "Epistles." [9] It is true that there is a very large coincidence of vocabulary in these documents. But it is equally true, and hardly less apparent, that the conceptions conveyed by the common words are very different. Most obvious is the conception of the paraclete. In this gospel the Holy Spirit is " another Paraclete "; in 1 John the Paraclete is Jesus Christ the Just. In the gospel the Paraclete is to be with the disciples forever; in 1 John he is with God. In the gospel the Paraclete is to lead the disciples into all the truth; in 1 John he is the propitiation for all sin. There are similarly comparable differences in the ideas about spirit in the two writings. The expectations about the end of the age differ. All these facts are significant in determining authorship.

What is most significant of all is not discussed in the handbooks. It is that the conception of religion held by the leaders who wrote the two sources differs fundamentally. In the " Epistles " we have another attempt to preserve the essential simplicities of a relatively primitive conception of Christianity. The type of the religious life is not that reflected by the gospel-making movement. The leader who wrote the " Epistles " is not a Scripturalist at all. There is not a single quotation of Scripture in the three sources. There is but one biblical allusion, the reference to Cain. This would not be surprising in the two brief letters, but it is surely not accidental in the case of the longer work. There is no quotation to prove anything because in the writer's conception of religious leadership Scripture as proof and sanction is gratuitous. His religion had no need for them in these ways.

He, like Paul and the writer of 1 Peter, was a spiritist. The point contrasts with the conception of religion held by the writer of the Fourth Gospel.

On the whole, it seems most satisfactory to agree with such a scholar as Dibelius that the Fourth Gospel and the " Johannine Epistles " were written by different persons. This involves, further, the abandonment of the ascription of any or all these writings to the shadowy "Elder John." It must frankly be acknowledged that it cannot be discovered who wrote these works.

As has been suggested, the point is not important. What is important is that from the " Epistles " much is learned of the growth of Christianity in the early decades of the second century, when problems were precipitated by the rise of sectaries. The great question was, could Christianity achieve the ideal of unity?

XII

EPISCOPAL CORRESPONDENCE

It has been mentioned that Ignatius, bishop of Antioch, wrote several letters while on his way as a prisoner to Rome. Six of these were to churches. One was to Polycarp, bishop of Smyrna. A number of their contributions to our knowledge of the religious life of the Christians of the early second century have been used to illustrate the " Johannine letters." Indeed, except for adverting to certain further details, it is unnecessary to discuss the letters to the churches at any greater length.

It is interesting, however, to note that the custom of inter-communication between churches by letter writing was fully used by Christian leaders and by Christian churches. Professor Goodspeed has fully discussed this phenomenon. That Paul wrote to churches is hardly more important than that an able leader saw the value of collecting and publishing his letters together for the benefit of all the churches. That the writer of Revelation followed this analogy by prefacing a general letter to letters to seven individual churches is an indication of the quick response which was accorded the publication of Paul's letters.

The custom of providing non-epistolary addresses with quasi-epistolary salutations and conclusions has been observed. We have seen the Roman church extending its influence in a long treatise which was cast in the form of a letter. We have seen a local bishop sending letters to an individual and to a church, and an address to a group of churches. The further letter writing of Ignatius and Polycarp throws additional light upon the intercommunication of Christian leaders and churches by letter writing.

What is first to be observed is that what was done by the collector of Paul's letters was done in this case in response to the impulse toward intercommunication. To be sure, there were now more evident reasons why it should have been done. There was now a general conception of the church as one widely diffused institution. Doubtless what Ignatius wrote had special value because it was known that he was a confessor-bishop on his way to martyrdom. But in any case it is significant that the bishop of a Syrian city was aware of, interested in, and desirous of instructing Asian churches. As shall be shown, in his letter to the individual, Polycarp, Ignatius has much to say that is directed to the larger group. And Polycarp obviously accepts the assumption that he may with propriety address as distant a church as that in Philippi.

Ignatius seems to have written his letters in groups. Evidently he was transported by the land route, so that he was taken through several of the cities to whose churches he wrote from a convenient central point. Probably after having visited the Ephesians, Magnesians and Trallians he wrote to these in retrospect from Smyrna. Likewise he wrote to the Philadelphians and the Smyrneans from Troas just before sailing for Neapolis. It would seem (Pol. 8:1) that it was not until after leaving Troas, perhaps from Philippi, that he wrote to Polycarp. He had written to the Romans, expecting his letter to precede his arrival, from Smyrna

(Rom. 10); the letter was doubtless carried by certain Christians who preceded him (Rom. 10:2).

Soon after they were written there was a strong impulse to collect Ignatius' letters. Polycarp says (Pol. 13), "Both you and Ignatius wrote to me that if anyone was going to Syria he should take your letters. . . . We send to you, as you requested, the letters of Ignatius which were sent to us by him and such others as we had with us. These are attached under this letter; you will be able to profit greatly from them. For they contain faith, stedfastness, and everything which builds up pertaining to our Lord." This remarkable witness to the thoroughness of the communication of the several churches with one another goes far to enable the understanding of Christianity's achievement of solidarity.

Ignatius' letter to Polycarp is, curiously enough, more general in its advice, although nominally addressed to an individual,[1] than are his letters to churches. The regular sequence of imperatives, typical in paraenesis, reminds one of the Epistle of James. It is important to note the problems discussed. While the matter of sectarian divisiveness, so prominent in his letters to churches, is alluded to, it is less prominent in the letter to the bishop. There is, however, a further example of the table of household duties, in which, as usual, the treatment of widows, slaves, women and men is taught. Following is a section containing Ignatius' favorite theme; the obedience of the bishop. Obviously this has no practical reference for Polycarp. It is addressed through him to the community, as is everything else in the letter, without doubt, except the purely personal matters.

One item is the reference of the confessor-bishop to his

erstwhile church. Ignatius had learned that Antioch has peace (i.e., is released from the pressure of the " persecution " which had claimed him as a victim), but he is none the less anxious for the Asians to establish contact with Antioch. To this end he recommends the calling of a common council, which shall select some trustworthy follower of Polycarp, whose duty it shall be to go to Syria " to glorify your (the pronoun is plural) zealous love to the glory of God." Other references to deputations to Syria occur; Ignatius wrote to the Philadelphians and the Smyrneans that they might properly send a deacon to Syria, remarking that neighboring churches have sent bishops, while others have sent presbyters and deacons. These data further indicate the solidarity of the Christian movement.

One detail of the achievement of unity, and thus the effecting of solidarity, is urged in the letter to Polycarp and in some of the letters to churches. It is the simple device of urging the multiplication of meetings: " Let the meetings (interestingly enough, the word is *synagoge,* certainly used in the non-technical sense) be held more often " is the advice to Polycarp (4:2) and to certain churches (Eph. 13:1; Mag. 7:2; cf. Eph. 5:3, 22:2).

Social problems are important in Ignatius' letter to Polycarp. The advice concerning slaves is an instance (4:3). The exhortation to treat them kindly hardly goes beyond the Pauline *Haustafel,* but Ignatius goes on to say (to the bishop) that the slaves must not be overweening. Indeed, the bishop of Antioch counsels the bishop of Smyrna to teach them to endure slavery to the glory of God, so that they may thus obtain a better freedom from God. It is inescapable that there had been agitation for freedom among Christian slaves. If this were not sufficiently proved by the reference just cited, it is established by the specific statement that slaves must not seek to be freed at the church's expense. Evidently there had been some practice of this kind of manumission.

Ignatius' references to Christian teaching must be noted. The most instructive is his statement about the gospel. Ignatius is a particularly compelling witness that the gospel was not merely *before* the gospels, but that gospel traditions persisted even *after* some of them were incorporated into written gospels. As an Antiochene, Ignatius was without doubt acquainted with the Matthean gospel. To him this was in some sense *the* gospel. Certainly the allusions which suggest Matthew outnumber those which indicate another gospel or the unidentifiable allusions. But there are surprising phenomena. For instance, coincidences with the Fourth Gospel are surprisingly frequent (Eph. 5:2; Mag. 7:2; Rom. 7:3; Philad. 7:1). Did Ignatius become acquainted with the Fourth Gospel while visiting the Asian churches? Was it to secure a sympathetic reading of his letters that he graciously wrote in its terms and figures? There is a reference to the resurrection appearances (Smyr. 3) which requires Luke-Acts or its basic tradition to satisfy it, while references to Paul and Peter as heroes (not dissimilar from those of 1 Clement) make his knowledge of Luke-Acts the more probable. Certainly Ignatius knew the corpus of Pauline letters; this is shown by his remark to the Ephesians that Paul " mentions them in every letter " (12:2).

However, the gospel allusions significantly appear without formula. Indeed, the only use of a formula (Eph. 5:3) is to introduce a Jewish Scripture (although secondarily it may reflect the New Testament works which quote the same source). Something definite is indicated by the words, "the ordinances of the Lord and of the apostles," or by "the ordinances of the apostles" (Mag. 13; Trall. 7:1). One wishes that the meaning were more specifically given. Certainly Ignatius did not mean the gospels and the writings of the apostles; this is shown indubitably by the full content of his statement. Likewise when he speaks of "the gospel" Ignatius has in mind the general meaning of the word, not some written document. This is shown, not merely by his figure of the gospel as "my refuge as the flesh of Jesus," but still more by his reference to the prophets who announced the gospel, and the summary statement about "the gospel of the common hope" (Philad. 5).

One must compare with these the statement, so tantalizing in its ambiguity, which was cited above: "I entreat you . . . to live according to Christian teaching (*kata christomathian*). For I heard certain men saying, 'If I do not find it in the archives (*archeiois*) I do not believe in the gospel,' and when I said to them that it has been written (*gegraptai*) they answered me, saying, 'That is just the question.' But to me the archives are Jesus Christ, the unchangeable archive is his cross, death, and resurrection and the faith which is through him" (Philad. 8:2).

Obviously the archives are definite and specific, but contain matter whose understanding was debatable. If, as the translation offered above suggests, the contrast is between the archives and the gospel (not the gospels, nor some one written gospel), the former might have been either Jewish Scripture generally speaking, or some such collection of messianic

proof-texts as that envisaged in Rendel Harris's *Testimonia*.[2]
This is to some extent suggested by the reference to the
prophets, the law of Moses and the gospel (Smyr. 5:1).

However, the ambiguity (which lies chiefly in the syntax
of the sentence) makes it possible that there is no such
dichotomy, but that the meaning is, " if I do not find it in
the charters, that is, in the gospel, I do not believe it." But
this would be opposed to everything else in Ignatius' conception of Christianity.

It is not essential to determine the exact meaning. It is
clear, in any case, that " the gospel " is not the same as the
gospels nor the equivalent of any one gospel. This is plainly
indicated in the statement: " But the gospel has certain pre-
eminence, that is, the appearance of the savior, our Lord
Jesus Christ, his suffering, and the resurrection. For the be-
loved prophets had a message pointing to him, but the gospel
is the perfection of incorruption " (Philad. 9). When it is
observed that the counterpart involved by the adversative
particle is a reference to priests and the high priest, the
meaning is clear: the gospel is superior to Jewish Scripture.
This is supported by Ignatius' warnings to beware of Jewish
propaganda and practice (Philad. 6:1; Mag. 8–10) and
made explicit in the remark that " the divine prophets
lived according to Jesus Christ " (Mag. 7:1). Ignatius sometimes speaks of the prophets in such a way as strongly to
suggest that he means the Christian prophets (cf. Smyr.
7:2; Philad. 5); certainly they are closely associated with
the gospel. It is all but certain that Ignatius means by the
gospel not the gospels but the content of the Christian message. The reference, already cited, to the ordinances of the
apostles bears this out; it is the whole message of the apostles,

not the writings of those represented in the New Testament, that is meant.

Two further considerations add probability to this. One is the statement about " the deacons [the term has technical meaning; it does not mean merely a male servant] of the mysteries of Jesus Christ " (Trall. 2:2). The other is the fact that among his additional distinctions Ignatius possessed the charism of inspired speech. Not only does he expect that the Lord will reveal things to him (Eph. 20:2), but he says that in one of his addresses he " cried out," and " spoke with a great voice, with God's voice," insisting that when he thus spoke he had no human knowledge of the matter of which he was speaking, but that it was the spirit who was preaching (Philad. 7). In Trallians 5 he further claims that highly spiritistic experiences were vouchsafed him. It is certain that to some degree Ignatius kept alive the Pauline type of experience, including the experience of ecstatic speech. This goes far to support the other evidence that he is one of the leaders who found some difficulty in allowing the gospels to displace the gospel.

There are no specific examples, comparable to those in 1 Clement, which indicate whether the gospel traditions were available to Ignatius as separate pericopes as well as in gospels and gospel sources. It is inherently possible. One consideration strongly suggests that his special problems actually led to the crystallization of gospel materials. This is the presence of quasi-creedal materials (Eph. 19:1; 20:1; Mag. 9; Trall. 9; Smyr. 1-2), in which clauses of confession appear in language which was later formulated into creeds. Undoubtedly the sectarian problems caused the articulation of these statements. The same forces caused the organization of gospel materials for defense against sectaries. Thus the emphasis upon such an item of the (later) gospel traditions as the true physical birth of Jesus, and such common items as his death and resurrection were essential in meeting the arguments of the "seemists." In these Ignatius illustrates processes which otherwise resulted in the formation of the gospels.

There is thus evidence that when Ignatius wrote, the gospel materials were still in evolution, not rigidly fixed by the writing of the gospels. Of course gospels had been written; not merely the four of the New Testament, but several, or even many, others. Likewise the gospel sources were still extant, both those used by the New Testament writers and others also. Without doubt there were still in circulation many "floating" pericopes, many stories and sayings, which never found their way into surviving documents. A possible instance of these materials in Ignatius is his reference to a miraculous star which shone at the birth of Jesus: "A star shone in heaven above all other stars; its light was unspeakable, and its newness caused astonishment. All other stars, with the sun and moon, gathered in choir around this star; it greatly exceeded all of them in its light. And there was perplexity about whence came this new thing, so out of the order of things" (Eph. 19:2).

Aware of many of these materials, it is not surprising that Ignatius means by "gospel" more than one or four gospels. He is another leader who takes from his treasure new things and old things, who uses traditions of Jesus which were parts of gospels, but who also has much more in his "gospel" than that which was written in gospels. Indeed, he can teach upon his own authority, even impressed by the analogy of the bishop and the Father (Trall. 3:1). Like Paul, he, too, in ecstasy has a direct and an immediate access to God and thus to divine teaching. Very much alive to the needs of the growing communities, he is greatly influenced by them in his articulations of Christian ways of life. In his conception of Christianity the church itself is a teacher. In an important sense it possessed the ordinances of the apostles. Its present officials mediated Christian teaching. Consequently Christian teaching for him was to be found in other sources than Scripture, although for him writings, Jewish and Christian, were part of the whole.

For some reason, Ignatius has not won the recognition which he merits.[3] His leadership, especially when it is compared with that of the writer of the Johannine letters, was promptly and firmly applied, as was necessary if any general solidarity of Christianity was to be achieved. Surely the forcefulness with which Ignatius met the situation, not merely in Syria but in the West, was highly effective in making second century Christianity what it became. Obviously Ignatius was a man of limited capability. It is also true that in his personal characteristics, showing themselves in his religious life, there were traits of abnormal psychic behavior. But he was bold, earnest and consistent. More of the ecclesiastical administrator than the creative leader, his lasting influence was on the side of organization rather than in blazing new trails.

Christianity appears as even more institutionalized in the letter which Polycarp, bishop of Smyrna, wrote to the Christians of Philippi.[4] This is perhaps because Polycarp exhibits a more disciplined and regimented mind than does Ignatius; it will not be forgotten that Ignatius, a thoroughly ecclesiastically minded bishop, kept alive the custom of charismatic speaking. While this distinction was claimed *for* Polycarp (*Martyrdom of Polycarp,* 12:1, 3, 16:2), it is not apparent in what he wrote. His letter abounds in Scriptural allusions, some of which are formally cited. The full range of ecclesiastical problems with which he deals, and the manner in which he meets them, show that he represented highly institutionalized religion.

These problems may be mentioned. From as early a source as Polycarp's letter it appears that money was an important consideration in church work. For Polycarp, using the epistolary address as a cloak, urges that the danger of the love of money is one which must be guarded against, and to this theme he again returns. It is discussed first in a general application, and then specifically directed to the " widows," i.e., those church workers technically so called, not including all women bereft of husbands, to the deacons, to the presbyters, and, negatively through the bad example of one Valens (a former presbyter) and his wife, who succumbed to temptation and made gain from their Christian work.

Second, Polycarp handles the family problem, urging that Christian wives be taught how they should live, while they, in turn, were thus to bring up their children. The " widows " are discussed next, then the deacons, whose qualifications are carefully listed, the younger men, and the presbyters, whose qualifications are also listed. Following some general exhortations, certain specific points are discussed, e.g., heresy; Polycarp was also troubled by the Docetists. It is evident, too, that the shadow of " persecution " constantly overhangs the Philippian group; many elements in Polycarp's letter are understandable only in view of this outlook. Doubtless this was the more relevant because Ignatius had recently passed through Philippi; Polycarp was sagacious enough to take full advantage of this fact in urging the value of steadfastness.

Polycarp writes, as he says, on the invitation of the Philippian church. Although he makes a studied depreciation of himself as compared with Paul, he maintains himself with dignity and authority. He associates elders with himself, but he is the teacher. He teaches in strictly moral terms; his churchmanship is highly sensitive ethically.

Polycarp's contribution to episcopal correspondence adds useful information concerning the effective intercommunication of early Christian groups. This appears from the fact that he writes in response to their invitation, in the fact that the immediate purpose of his writing is that of collecting the letters of Ignatius, and in certain details of the correspondence. For instance, it is clear that the Philippians had been forewarned of the coming of Ignatius and his party, so that they were prepared to meet them and send them on their way with assistance. Further, the Philippians and Ignatius had urged that persons going to Syria should take as many of Ignatius' letters as might be collected to his former diocese. Polycarp replies that he is sending someone to represent the Philippians and himself and will send as many letters as he can find. These, and others which he had, he sends to the Philippians also. A third fact is that there was information in common about Valens and his wife. Fourth, a number of problems are handled in such a manner as to show that they were common, rather than limited to a single church, so that the details are well known to Polycarp and to his readers. It is to be further noted that Polycarp is acquainted with 1 Peter, the baptismal address turned into an "epistle."

The last remark introduces the observation that Polycarp is well informed of the contents of Scripture, including a large number of Christian writings. He knew all of Paul's letters, which, judging from the fact that the number includes "Ephesians," he knew as a corpus. He makes those tantalizing remarks about Paul's "letters" (*sic*) to the Philippians (3:2, 11:3), thus furnishing objective ground for the inference required by internal evidence that our Philippians is composite. He knows several gospels, including Luke-Acts, and once he quotes by the formula, "remembering what the Lord taught when he said": unfortunately it is not possible to ascertain whether he thus cites Matthew, Luke-Acts, or a current form of floating logia. Polycarp certainly regards the gospel as the messages of the apostles, for he speaks of what Christ "commanded us, as he did the apostles, who brought us the gospel, and the prophets [i.e., the Jewish prophets] who foretold the coming of the Lord." As has been remarked, he knows 1 Peter. The reference to heresy is usually taken to indicate that he knows and quotes the Johannine letters, but his reference is such as to make it possible to regard it as his own observation, for the problem was a common one. But there is no reason to doubt that he knew these writings.

The major problem of Polycarp's knowledge of Christian writings is the question whether he knew and used the so-called Pastoral Epistles. Not only the importance of the problem, but its bearing upon consequent historical reconstruction, is involved. Obviously if Polycarp's letter is found to allude to the Pastorals it would require their dating at a time earlier than his letter. But it is the view of this study that the contents of Polycarp's letter which seem to reflect the Pastorals are similar to these because both deal with a common problem. If it were required to conclude that these similarities imply relationship, it would be necessary, according to the view of the present study, to affirm that it is the Pastorals which allude to Polycarp, rather than that Polycarp quotes the Pastorals.

A fuller statement of this judgment is advisable. It was pointed out that Polycarp as a church leader found it necessary to offer instruction (ostensibly to the Philippians, but actually in broader scope) concerning the qualifications of church workers. If these criteria are carefully compared with the treatment of the same matters in the Pastorals, one gains the impression that Polycarp's is the earlier of the two discussions. His is the more elementary, the less detailed, and suggestive of a less advanced stage in the definition of standards for the controlled selection of church workers. It is a fair inference that if Polycarp were here quoting the Pastorals his use would have been more extensive, while if the Pastorals use Polycarp the relationship would presumably be that which is indicated in the difference between the two sources. However, it is much the more probable that in this matter there is no literary relation at all, but that Polycarp and the author of the Pastoral Epistles deal independently with the common problem.

The second factor which is usually cited is the similarity of certain statements in the two sources. The most striking of these is in Polycarp 4:1: " But the first [chief, principal] of all evils is the love of money. Knowing, then, that we brought nothing into the world, neither have we anything to take out, let us arm ourselves. . . ." This resembles the well-known statement to the effect that the love of money is the root of all evils, etc., in the Pastorals. But the similarity is apparent only in English; in Greek the differences, particularly in Polycarp's first sentence, are telling: the words for " root " (in the Pastorals) and for " first " (chief, principal) (in Polycarp) are different; the words for " evil " are different in the two sources, and 1 Timothy uses the copula and the article with the word for " love of " money. Inasmuch as the saying is quasi-proverbial, and inasmuch as there is an Old Testament source for the saying about the impossibility of taking anything out of the world (Job 1:21), not much can be adduced to prove literary dependence of Polycarp upon the Pastorals, or vice versa.

On the whole, the most instructive view of the Epistle of Polycarp is to regard it as a source for the study of Christianity in Asia as it had grown in the second decade of the second century. When it is so used it exhibits just the growth from what is found in 1 Peter that the phenomena of the Johannine and the Ignatian letters would suggest. That is to say, Christianity was succeeding in establishing itself in the Roman world by effecting its own internal organization. Less creative than in earlier stages of its growth, it is more certain of permanent existence. For this its leaders deserve much credit. Such sensitiveness to the problems of venality, and such moral earnestness as one finds in Polycarp's letter indicate strong leadership. As the episcopal correspondence of Ignatius and Polycarp is studied the bishops appear as men of limited capabilities, but as men who make the most of the abilities which they have. As one sees, further, that standards for the measurement of the workers in the churches are emerging, one looks from the several problems which the episcopal administrators handle to the particular aspects involved in the growth of church rules.

XIII

THE GROWTH OF CHURCH RULES

In the decades after the gospel-making period the churches emerged to a more obvious position of authority. At the same time their problems correspondingly grew. No sooner did an able ecclesiastical leader appear than administrative and moral questions faced him. As the church achieved a conception of its corporate greatness, forces appeared which threatened to prevent the successful assertion of central control. Because some aspects of the religious life were neglected by some leaders in certain sections, religious groups appeared which emphasized the neglected aspects and from the ensuing issue many were attracted to sectarian trends.

Internal developments occurred similarly. Patterns of the life of the church member became regularized or even conventionalized. Tasks of church workers became specialized and thus capable of definition and of detailed standardization. It was now possible to specify the duties of officials. Yet at the same time it was necessary to see that the religious life of the people conformed to the patterns which were deemed right by their leaders. It became necessary to test the officials by imposing the prescriptions of their offices. It became equally necessary to insure that the workers properly discharged their duties as to specify the duties with which they were entrusted. In every case advance corresponded with the complexity of the situation.

It is possible to see how some of these situations developed. Thus the writer of 1 Peter found it necessary to add to the main theme of his address his judgment concerning what seems already to have become a perplexing, as it proved to be a persistent, problem: the exploitation of church office for private gain. This was, as has been seen, an important matter when Polycarp wrote to the Philippians; it seems to have been the cause of the downfall of Valens and his wife, and the repeated admonitions of the bishop to various officials suggest that it was a widespread danger.

The growth and the specialization of the work of the church officials furnishes a second illustration. By the time that Ignatius wrote to Polycarp the status of " widows " as church workers appears. These were recognized church workers with specific duties. It goes without saying that by this time differentiation of the work of deacons and elders had occurred, at least in some localities.[1] It is a matter of no practical importance whether this involved the emergence of a church order of government which was uniform or even general; the type of church order differed in particular places and times. It is of even less importance whether bishops, elders and deacons represented three " orders " of ministry or two. What is important is that in the period of Christianity's emerging maturity the specialization of the religious life and task necessarily caused the work of the officials to differentiate. It is likely that in the inchoate Christianity of earlier periods there were workers whose duties even though they were known are not reported as they are in later sources. But it is certain that as the aggressive spread of Christianity in the larger world met with large popular response, it became necessary to articulate the specific duties of the workers. This was, in fact, a phase of Christianity's maturing.

Nowhere do these facts appear more plainly than in the so-called Pastoral Epistles. When these sources are properly used their information is voluminous and clear. Unfortunately, they are seldom properly used. They cannot give their information about the religious life of the Christians in their period as long as they are studied to prove that Paul wrote them, or that they contain genuine Pauline sources. Nothing but a thoroughly inductive approach to them suffices. Nothing is plainer than that the contents of the Pastorals do not fit any situation of Paul's lifetime. The difference between these and the Pauline letters includes not only difference of vocabulary and style, but difference of religious conceptions and the actual life of the Christians. Hence a discussion which begins with the arguments designed to establish Pauline authorship and situation neglects the features which are distinctive. For the same reason a work which addresses itself to the proof that the Pastorals contain genuine Pauline sources or fragments means that these are considered the valuable parts of the letters, with consequent neglect of the really considerable elements.[2]

The inductive approach first undertakes to find from the data of the letters the situation which called them forth. This includes, of course, the discovery of their occasion. These data are what make it impossible to find a situation and an occasion for them in anything which can be known of the lifetime of Paul. To be sure, one form of the "Ephesian imprisonment" hypothesis has the detailed feature that the Pastorals may thus be viewed as coming from the "second imprisonment,"[3] that in Rome referred to in the last verses of Luke-Acts. But this is no more reasonable, nor as reasonable, as the older hypothesis that Paul was released from a " first " imprisonment in Rome, that he engaged in missionary activity such as is reflected in the Pastorals, and then wrote these from a " second " Roman imprisonment from which he was not released. But it is simply not possible to discover such a situation as the Pastorals depict at any time nor in any place in the first century. To be sure, the source theory of P. N. Harrison makes it possible to look merely to a few fragments for data of Paul's situation, and thus to relate everything else to the situation of the " editor " of the Pastorals. But this merely restates the same fundamental question: what was the situation?

The situation of the Pastorals involves elements which are corollaries of the data commonly viewed. Among these is the use of Paul's name. Why did a Christian ecclesiastic, writing at some time in the second century, representing thereby a certain point of view, make his points by using the aegis of Paul's name?

In considering the pseudonymity of the Pastorals it is profitable to regard the growth of Christianity in the Pauline circles subsequent to Paul's death. One finds that current Christianity in these localities had completely changed. It was thoroughly un-Pauline. To be sure, the new view of the origin and function of the corpus of Paul's letters shows that Paul was used in a certain institutional way. But Paul never thought that these churches would be in existence as late as the time that the Pastorals were written, whatever that time was. The view of a general or a catholic church, which was expected to be quasi-permanent in its establishment, was never envisaged by Paul. The articulation of definite stand-

ards and duties of workers and officials stands in stark contrast with the dependence upon spiritual gifts in genuinely
Pauline Christianity.

Likewise the development of Christian teaching was along
lines foreign to Paul's religion. Not only does the process
differ, but the social basis of Christian didactic was un-Pauline.
The emergence of general patterns was the result of processes
utterly antithetical to Paul's " teaching." The development
of codes which were standards to measure the propriety
or the peculiarity of one's belief was a vastly different
process.

It was inevitable, of course, that the infinite variety, implicit in the trust in spiritistic experience, made for the
development of other types of experience as soon as Paul and
other vigorous leaders passed from the scene. In any case,
the formerly Pauline churches developed in other than
Pauline directions. As shall be shown presently, certain implications of Paul's ways of the religious life are to be seen
in operation at later dates, but it is nevertheless true that in
the very places where he had founded churches Paul, after
his death, was not followed in what he had taught.

It is often said that Paul, so to speak, went into an eclipse
during the first half of the second century. The evidence
for this view is that such a Christian leader as Justin Martyr
does not mention his name (although he exhibits thorough
acquaintance with his writings). The usual explanation is
that the use made of Paul by the heretic Marcion made it
politic for orthodox leaders to refrain from mentioning him.
To be sure, Justin's failure to cite Paul's name is balanced by
its honorific use by Ignatius and Polycarp. But it is relevant
and entirely fair to raise the question of the relation of Mar-

cion and his movement to other aspects of early Christianity during the time of its emerging maturity.

It is possible that Marcion and his movement may be of assistance in discovering the situation and the occasion of the Pastorals. It is advisable to set forth certain essential facts.[4]

Marcion was a man whose home was in Sinope, a seaport city of Pontus. Probably he was a convert to Christianity, rather than a child of a Christian home. He became a wealthy man. Apparently he had some education. At all events, he was a capable thinker who exercised acute abilities in his religious life. He studied and reflected upon religious literature. The result of these activities was his development of certain judgments which did not agree with those commonly held by Christian leaders. As fruits of his distinctive reflection he produced a system of teaching and a book. It is regrettable that it cannot be determined whether these developments occurred while Marcion was living in Sinope or afterward. For by the year 139 he was in Rome, where he established contact with the local Christians. He made a large gift of money to the Roman church. While he was in Rome his ideas and teachings met with opposition from church leaders. He was finally deemed to be heterodox in his beliefs and since he persisted in disseminating them he was expelled from the church as a heretic. At this time the equivalent of his gift to the church was returned to him. This had occurred not later than the year 144. Since the subsequent history of Marcion and Marcionism do not concern the present study, nothing more needs to be said, except to remark that the Marcionite movement attained considerable influence by the middle of the second century. It persisted for some time.

Marcion's ideas may be briefly stated. He thought that Christianity as generally understood was a perversion of true Christianity. Paul, he thought, had been the only one who had correctly apprehended the significance of Jesus. Marcion denied the validity of the Jewish elements in the Christian tradition, teaching and institutions. Basic to his judgment was a thoroughgoing study of the nature of God. Marcion was a radical dualist. He found it impossible to believe that the God of Jewish teaching could have been the God of Jesus. Thus he insisted that true Christianity involved the rejection of all elements derived from Jewish sources.

This involved a criticism of Scripture. Needless to say, nothing in Jewish Scripture survived Marcion's analysis. The development of his points brought about a number of details which are coincident with other systems called by modern scholars gnosticism. But Marcion's system was hardly a gnosis, although it has affinities with gnostic teachings. For one thing, Marcion's view was not abstract. He was a thoroughly practical person, whose ideas were offered in no doctrinaire spirit. To be sure, his system was shaped in terms of a series of emanations from deity, with the active agent the so-called demiurge. This, in turn, led to the statement of cosmological ideas in which, again, similarities with gnostic systems are obvious.

Naturally such divergences from usual Christianity led to the treatment of Marcion as a sectary and a heretic. But it must be insisted that the basic elements of his leadership were not intellectual but practical. For example, probably the achievement which more than anything else put him beyond the pale was his biblical criticism. Marcion completely rejected Jewish Scripture. More than this, he handled the generally accepted Christian writings very radically. He was the first Christian leader to organize Christian writings as a Scripture. In other words, he was the first to put forth a New Testament. He did this by taking the Lucan gospel (which was probably already separated from the Acts section of Luke-Acts) and the letters of Paul, editing them, and using them as Scripture. This led to a storm of opposition,[5] for this was an institutional, rather than a doctrinal matter.

A number of relevant factors are brought to light by this recital of the salient features of the work of Marcion. One is that it shows the existence of a clear-cut division between the practice and the theory of Christianity on the Jewish question. Practically this question had long since been settled, essentially on the lines of Marcion's judgment. Christianity was and had long been a gentile religion, with its character determined by gentile features. It was the rigorous application of Marcion's logic, rather than any fundamental disagreement with his theology, which caused the break between Marcion and other churchmen. Probably the practical difference in their use of Scripture was less significant than the strict application of his views to the point of tampering with the church's Scripture. And yet, more regular churchmen than Marcion had been driven to curious lengths to make many parts of Scripture meaningful, practical and useful. As the Epistle of Barnabas shows,[6] the allegorical method of interpretation, long since used in Alexandria and elsewhere,[7] had been appropriated for this purpose. Only the use of this method of interpreting Scripture, particularly Jewish Scripture, made it possible for Christians to relate the

Jewish elements of their religion to the more characteristic elements, and thus to make a comprehensive whole of the heterogeneous parts.

As all the sources of the period show, many leaders were thinking about the nature of God, for a number of reasons and purposes. Some wished to furnish Christianity with an adequate intellectual basis. Some, attracted by the implications of the dualistic philosophies, were working out reflections on the nature of God in the direction taken by the gnostic teachers. Some were content to reiterate the traditional theologies.

Several leaders, as the sources show, were busy in stating the essentials about the nature of religion and of the church. These were, however, practical interests, taking the direction of disciplinary questions. The duties of workers and officials were more pressing problems in these situations than were the questions about what officials ought to believe. Religion was operating satisfactorily as long as the problems of the cult members were kept within the narrow sphere of personal relations, so that essential simplicities were not disturbed.

These were important factors when the writer of the Pastorals produced these works which he ascribed to Paul. Evidently the most pressing of them was the necessity of controlling the members and the officials of the churches as the members increased in number and the duties of the officials correspondingly increased in complexity and responsibility. It is a human scene which appears in these " letters." When it is necessary to stipulate that women must dress modestly, without wearing jewelry, without dressing their hair fashionably, and without wearing costly clothing or ornaments;

when one must exhort that men must refrain from anger and argument; when it must be required that the overseer of a church must be no brawler, no striker, no fighter and no lover of money; when it must be insisted that the deacons be not given to the frequent use of wine nor greedy for dirty money, the implications are plain. It is apparent that Christianity is growing rapidly, so rapidly that there is a danger that the numerous adherents cannot be assimilated without themselves dominating the movement. The need for workers has brought the danger that grossly unfit persons will be put in places of responsibility. Surely the requirements for officials are sufficiently modest, not to say elementary.

Specialization of religious work is plain. The statements about the widows show this. The churches had assumed the responsibility of caring for these women, and those who were so cared for were given some status as workers. These, not all women bereft of husbands, are the " widows " of Ignatius, Polycarp and the Pastorals. Obviously these women became a problem, and one can see how the problem grew in complexity as one passes from the earlier to the later of these sources. A cause of the problem was the fact that there were so many of the widows. The writer of the Pastorals therefore recommends that only women who are unlikely to marry again should be considered as " widows "; strangely enough he determines this probability by arbitrarily ruling that such a woman sixty years of age might be listed as a widow, while one younger might not! The younger women might be expected to marry, and this would be best for them. Yet this distinction between them does not suffice, for it is urged that whenever possible the children or the grandchildren should care for widowed relatives. Only those not otherwise taken care of would be enrolled among the church workers.

There are still other simple and homely tests of the legitimacy of widows: they must have been married only once, must be of good reputation, must be mothers who have successfully brought up children, must have practiced hospitality and have frequently entertained stranger Christians, and in this must have done the usual acts such as washing their feet and nursing in case of illness. Practical experience has taught the writer that not all widows could meet these tests, for he fears that the younger ones will be idle, neighborhood gossips, and persons whose behavior will get them and the church into disrepute.

The leader whose judgments are given in the Pastorals sets up only very practical tests of church workers. This appears from the simple and elementary criteria by which they are to be judged. The overseers, or bishops, must, like the widows, be of good repute, temperate (there is special warning against addiction to drink), sensible, well behaved, hospitable, competent to teach, not in the habit of getting into drunken fights, not lovers of money. They must be men who have demonstrated their ability to maintain order in their homes. It is especially significant that they must be well thought of outside the churches.

While the deacons are of lower rank than the overseers, two standards are recited which are also required of overseers: they must not be overindulgent in their use of wine, and they must not be greedy for dirty money. Deacons must survive a period of probation, during which they must demonstrate their abilities to meet these standards. This precautionary measure enabled the churches to maintain another standard held by the writer of the Pastorals: the churches must not ordain their officials hastily. Using a technical term, it is directed that the overseer must not be a mere novice.

To be sure, there are religious standards for the workers. The overseers are expected to be just, consecrated and self-controlled, committed to the message which can be relied on, exactly as they were taught. The deacons must hold the mystery of the faith in a pure conscience. But it is notable that more attention is paid to the elemental moral qualifications than to the religious.

What seems to be the most important consideration is the matter of money. More than once it is insisted that no one may become a church worker of whom it can be said that he is a lover of money. It is recognized that this qualification is necessary because some of the officials have been lovers of money and have used their offices for personal gain. It is highly significant, in view of these things, that in the situation of the Pastorals the church workers are paid. This is unmistakably shown in the statement that elders who do their work well, particularly those who work at preaching and teaching, are actually worth twice what they get.

Of course the question of money involved others than the church workers. While the attitude toward wealth in the Pastorals is by no means that which is found in Luke-Acts and the homily of James, it is apparent that these writings reflect a problem created by the fact that the churches now included wealthy persons as members. All members are warned that godliness together with contentment is a superior state, inasmuch as no one can take wealth with him when he dies. None the less, it is observed, the desire to be rich causes many temptations, and evil often comes of it; the love of money is the root of all evil things. But the rich people are a special object of solicitude. They are to be warned against being arrogant, but to do good with their wealth, sharing it generously. It is most instructive to note the emphasis upon the problems resulting from wealth in the different conceptions of the writers of Luke-Acts, Hermas, 1 Peter, James, Polycarp and the Pastorals. The Christian movement no longer drew its public only from among the poor. It now numbered no few of the rich among its adherents.

A corollary may be asserted. With the inclusion of wealthy persons, it is probable that Christianity achieved a higher degree of respectability than it had previously enjoyed. Certainly the Pastorals reflect the desirability of possessing the good repute of outsiders.

This is an essential clew, also, to the understanding of the intellectual aspects which are important in the Pastorals. When Christianity became inclusive of rich persons it also reached a higher intellectual status. Not that the rich were intellectuals, but that wealth, although it is but one, is an important element in cultural status. Necessarily the intellectual aspects of Christianity appeared relatively late. They had appeared when the Pastorals were written.

Doubtless the necessity to develop intellectual aspects was forced upon the Christian movement from the outside. In large part the rise of heretical movements was due to the slowness with which Christianity developed intellectually; it was unable to give leadership and encouragement, much less stimulation, to those of its number who had intellectual aptitudes, so that it became practically necessary for these to express themselves outside the church. This phenomenon appears in the Pastorals. One of the critical problems which they reflect is that sectaries worm their way among the members, particularly among the women, and entice them toward interest in wrong teaching (2 Tim. 3:6).

Almost all of the items alluded to in the Pastorals which refer to heretical teaching conform to the known characteristics of Marcionite teaching. Some correspond closely; some cannot be viewed as related to Marcion's ideas. Those which are obviously different are the references to Jews who make trouble (Titus 1:10, 14), and to teaching which involves the use of Scripture in a way which was incompatible with Marcion's views (1 Tim. 1:7-9; Titus 3:9). However, these may be merely fictitious allusions designed to gain verisimilitude for the writings by introducing references suggestive of a Pauline situation. A more important item is the reference to individual teachers, not otherwise known, who allege that the resurrection had already occurred (2 Tim. 2:18); this does not suggest Marcionism. There are also certain general references which are not identifiable as aspects of any known sectarian group.

But certain items strikingly suggest the Marcionite situation. "There is only one God, and one intermediary between God and man, the man Christ Jesus, who gave himself as a ransom for all men" (1 Tim. 2:5). If this is not a shaft at Marcion's distinction between the just God and the creator God it is a most unusual coincidence. The statement about men "who forbid people to marry, and insist on abstinence from certain kinds of food that God created . . . for everything that God created is good" (4:3f.) is particularly relevant against the background of Marcionite controversy; the oft-quoted prescription that Timothy should drink a little wine may be of the same interest. The rhetorical doxology of 1 Tim. 6:15f. has particular meaning as an anti-Marcionite assertion.

Effective as anti-Marcionite propaganda, whether this is expressed or merely implied, is the famous statement of 2 Timothy 3:16: " All Scripture is divinely inspired, and is useful. . . ." The insistence that *all* Scripture is divinely inspired and useful has the utmost significance when viewed as a repudiation of Marcion's well-known distinction between Scripture which taught what he considered to be truth and Scripture which taught what he conceived to be error. The emphasis upon *all* Scripture as against some is particularly relevant in that Marcion limited, while the general church fully included, the content of Scripture. It must be emphasized that the decisive element in Marcion's use of Scripture was that he ventured to tamper with an already ancient institution. This was much more reprehensible than was the fact that he promulgated unusual views. The spokesman for the church must defend her institutions.

Last to be mentioned is a datum which may be most striking of all. First Timothy concludes with advice to " guard that which has been entrusted to you. Keep away from the worldly, empty phrases and the antitheses of the falsely so-called gnosis, through professing which some have made a failure of the faith " (6:20f.). Is it only a coincidence that the language of the statement uses the very term which was used in the title of Marcion's theological treatise, the *Antitheses*? The suggestion that it is actually an allusion to Marcion's work has been made by as serious a scholar as Harnack.[8] Few scholars have been hospitable to the suggestion; in most cases because it entails a late date for the Pastorals. Certainly the coincidence, if it is only a coincidence, is extraordinary. Even apart from the one term the statement as a whole perfectly suits a situation in which Marcion or Marcionism is being attacked. The reference strongly supports the others to the same effect.

It may therefore be said that these, together with other data of the Pastorals, point to a situation late enough in time and of such particular character (whatever the place may be) which reflects the rise of Marcionism as the dominant element.

The mention of the statement that all Scripture is divinely inspired and useful makes it relevant to allude further to this important item. A minimum of reflection suffices to show that it assumes the allegorical method of interpretation. This method had long since been used in Greek localities, and was particularly current in Alexandria. Its use by Alexandrian Jewish scholars is familiar. It importantly affected the translation of Jewish Scripture commonly called the Septuagint. Its most famous exponent, Philo, used it prolifically. That the method was adopted by Christians is not surprising. It may be observed in what is generally considered to be a work which reflects Alexandria, the Epistle to the Hebrews. It is to be found in a particular form in the Fourth Gospel, which has allegories instead of parables.

But the work which is the classic example of Christian use of allegorical method of interpreting Scripture is the so-called Epistle of Barnabas. This perfectly illustrates the manner by which all Scripture was found to be divinely inspired and useful. The inspiration, even though it was not apparent, could always be found, granted that the interpreter had sufficient ingenuity. This sort of inspiration made the most unpromising Scripture useful for any purpose toward which the interpreter worked.

In this light Barnabas is an illuminating commentary on the Pastorals. They are, of course, dissimilar in many ways. But in their conception of Christianity, and particularly in their conception of the Christian task, the one aids in the understanding of the other. Both are fundamentally un-Jewish; both are actually hostile to Judaism. But both appropriate Jewish values which they use in anti-Jewish propaganda. Of these the most conspicuous is, of course, Jewish Scripture — the Pastorals use even Jewish apocrypha — which is made to serve Christian and anti-Jewish purpose by pragmatic interpretation. It is clear, as the Pastorals and Barnabas are studied, that the latter aids in placing the former in their situation and in discovering their objective and occasion.

These factors should prepare the student for the judgment that the Pastorals emerge in the definite period of Christianity's maturing. If there is no discoverable place for them in the lifetime of Paul, and if theories of genuine Pauline elements are recognized as essentially useless, there is no alternative.

It is sometimes said that the date of the Pastorals is fixed by their use by Polycarp in his letter. Evidence has been given to show that the alleged parallels are not convincing, and to show that such as they are they are readily explicable as common epigrammatic sayings. Or, as was pointed out, it would be equally defensible to assert that the Pastorals depend upon Polycarp.

The use of Paul's name in the " letters " aids further in

discovering the situation of the Pastorals. The alleged "eclipse" of Paul in the early second century has been referred to. The usual view is that Paul lost caste because of Marcion's use of him. However this may be, it must be recognized that the eclipse of Paul was not as complete as is usually supposed. Professor Goodspeed has shown that the collection of Paul's letters placed these in a central position of ecclesiastical use. First Clement, Ignatius and Polycarp unite in exalting Paul's heroic reputation. These facts require heavy discount of the idea that Paul suffered an eclipse. If the appearance of the Pastorals is placed as next in this sequence, their writer must be viewed as doing a thing whose significance was all the greater when placed against the background of emerging Marcionism. It was a strategic thing for the writer of the Pastorals to combat Marcionite propaganda by presenting counter-teaching in the name of Paul. If Paul had lost in the estimation of certain Christian leaders, or if he had been rendered less available for use in common Christian teaching, because Marcion was thought to have distorted his teaching, this use of his name did much to rehabilitate him.

Barnabas may be referred to in this connection also. The Marcionite view was one of the logical positions forced by the relation of Christianity to Judaism. The opposite position was taken by "Barnabas," in which Jewish Scripture is used by understanding it figuratively. This was the issue: a Christian leader might logically abandon the Jewish Scripture altogether, or he might use it in ways not at all intended by it. Allegory made this possible. The Scylla of the Jewish view and the Charybdis of Marcion's logic were thus alike avoided by Barnabas — and the Pastorals — by the use of allegory. In this way institutionally minded leaders were able to preserve Jewish Scripture, and were able to make some practical use of it; at the same time they were relieved of the embarrassment occasioned by the many things which it plainly says. One of these leaders proceeded in this way, writing an " epistle " under the name of Barnabas; another wrote three " letters " under the name of Paul.

It is not suggested that the coincidence of the Pastorals and Barnabas is complete. Each had its own task, which each met in its own way. However, it is worth pointing out that the didactic element, much the more fully developed in Barnabas, is clearly related to the general situation which is discovered in these later books of the New Testament. Having literary relations with the teacher's code which is represented in the *Didache,* and drawing much from literary sources, e.g., the " Two Ways " document also used in the *Didache,*[9] largely depending upon Jewish Scripture, Barnabas presents Christian teaching as a " new Law " (2:6). This indicates that while the work exhibits knowledge and use of at least the Matthean gospel, its conception of religious teaching is by no means that in which the gospel type of writing is exclusively or even primarily used. If there is a difference between Barnabas and the Pastorals at this point it is the difference between Asia (or Rome) and Alexandria.

Neither do the Pastorals suggest exclusive or primary dependence upon the type of tradition represented in the familiar gospels. The function of the " Faithful Sayings " clearly proves this; the distinctive formula, used five times, has its root in another tradition. Equally significant are the distinctive references to Jesus. These reflect the growing tradition which resulted — at about this time, be it noted —

in the production of " apocryphal " gospels. " Apocryphal "
gospels, it will be remembered, were merely stories of Jesus
on a more thoroughly popular level than the four which more
conservative tradition brought into common and presently
exclusive use in the churches. It is thus that the hymn of 1
Timothy 3:16 is to be viewed, with its references to Jesus as
" manifested in flesh, pronounced just by spirit, seen by
angels, heralded among the nations, believed by the world,
ascended in glory." Not all these items can be satisfied by
elements in the four gospels. Again, the reference to Jesus
in 2 Timothy 2:8 is very like the growing creed as it was seen
in the Ignatian Epistles. It is doubtful that 1 Timothy
6:13–16 is the fruit of the four gospel tradition merely. And
2 Timothy 1:9f has the appearance of typical apocrypha.

It is to the same effect that the Pastorals abound in data
by which legend enriches the figure of Paul. Many such
have contributed to Paul's heroic stature in tradition. It is
instructive to observe this phenomenon operating in Christianity at this time. Providing Paul with heroic stature, particularly by picturing him as a martyr, is the very thing
done in and by " apocryphal acts " literature, in which every
apostle must be a hero and nearly everyone die a martyr's
death. That this interest was served by the Pastorals conclusively demonstrates the point to which Christianity had
developed when they were written.

In fine, the Pastorals exhibit not merely an advanced Christianity, a Christianity with a controlled officiary, a Christianity with a well-developed content of belief, but a Christianity which is conscious of diversity within itself and able
and ready to invoke the available criteria to determine the
regularity of discipline and the orthodoxy of belief. The

Pastorals are understood when they are viewed against the background of Marcion and his sectarian movement. It is probable that their background is the early Marcionism of Asia Minor, as it was before Marcion came to Rome; it is emerging Marcionism, rather than the full-fledged theological Marcionism.

When they are so viewed the Pastoral Epistles become a highly important source for the knowledge of Christianity in a vital situation and at a critical time. It is of slight importance to determine the name of a " heresy " or to cite its tenets. But it is instructive to observe how the general and a minority Christian movement function in meeting religious needs, and to discover how the one group precipitates problems of discipline for the other. This example exhibits Christianity as faced with an inevitable consequence of its diversity and its failure to give sufficient place to the expression of intellectual aspects of its religious life.

The Pastorals were faced with their sectarian problems because most Christian leaders had chosen to subordinate emphasis upon intellectual elements, even though this occasioned the growth of popular movements which arose in response to this neglect.

In the main, the movement which became Christianity met with success because it was popular and inclusive. But it was presently unable to include within itself certain groups which persisted in keeping the particularly intellectual interests in the foreground. Forceful leaders representing these as primary interests developed minority groups which in turn became genuinely social movements. In the beginning they were all within the bounds of the general " Christian " movement. But when leaders who were also forceful, but who emphasized other interests as primary, failed to recognize these as genuine social movements, and thereupon attempted to draw lines of regularity, discipline and correctness of belief, the inevitable result was the precipitation of tendencies into actual sects and heretical movements.

One learns much of the technique of control from the Pastorals. Ecclesiastical leaders accepted the issue from minority groups, and proceeded to maintain control by treating them as outsiders. Whether because of inadequate intellectual capacity, or because of a deliberate disregard of the intellectual aspects of the religious life, such leaders set up minimum standards to which the adherents of the movement must conform. Probably much more was lost than was gained by so doing. The validity of government through church rule was preserved, but the consequent impoverishment of judgment on the one hand and the deliberate sacrifice of variant judgment and richer intellectual expression on the other hand were results of serious moment for the future of the general movement.

XIV

MATURING CHRISTIANITY

If it seems strange to suggest that Christianity was maturing by the time that the mid-point of the second century was reached it must be remembered that Christianity had a remarkably rapid development. It will not seem strange to the student who views the growth of Christianity with perspective. It has been a basic point of view in the present study that such a perspective is furnished by Christianity's writings. The fact becomes clear when one reflects that "Christianity" had nearly twenty years of expansion before any of its extant writings appeared, that a single leader produced several writings of which nine are extant in less than ten years, that several gospel sources, at least four gospels, and three non-gospel writings appeared in the next thirty years, and that the next fifty years saw the appearance and survival of twenty-five or more works of several different types.[1] One must remember also that the latest books of the New Testament are contemporaneous with the literature of defense represented by the political and cultural apologies,[2] that by this time the "apocryphal" gospels flourished,[3] and that the martyrologies soon after were popular.[4] One then sees that Christianity's maturity is indicated by its writings.

Doubtless the strangeness in the suggestion obtains because the writings of the New Testament are usually considered by themselves, apart from the "non-canonical" writings. It is high time that the abstraction, the distinction between New Testament and extra-New Testament sources be abandoned. All sources are useful for the study of the religious life of the early Christians.

Indeed, such works as the Epistle of Jude and 2 Peter cannot be understood unless they are studied as products of maturing Christianity, and are studied on the basis of contemporary sources.

When they are so studied, they are readily understood and appreciated. Their major problems are simple, given the background of maturing Christianity. The manner in which they met their problems is simple. The primary point is that which was common from the time that the unnamed elder asserted his authority against Diotrephes; indeed, it was not unknown before — the problem of control of minority groups within the general Christian movement.

For the writer of Jude the problem was precipitated by persons who had sneaked into the group and were using their privilege of membership to develop among the group practices which were repugnant. To the writer these practices are positively immoral.

It is interesting that heretical teachings were not the most important element in this sectarian problem. Perhaps this is because " Jude " is not distinguished as an intellectual leader.

He meets his problem, not by demonstrating the errors of the sectaries, but by calling them names, trusting that the use of effective epithets will cancel their influence. Very likely it did; this method has always been used by majority leaders, and it came to be characteristic of orthodox leadership.

It is of prime importance that Jude as leader of the majority group appeals to authority to establish his case. His authority is Scripture and "the words spoken before by the apostles." He is catholic in his use of Scripture, alluding to standard Jewish writings and also to two books which are Scripture to him, although their status was uncertain to many Jews, i.e., the *Assumption of Moses* and some form of the book of *Enoch*. Doubtless Jude was an ardent apocalyptist, although the brevity of his "epistle" does not permit him to expound this aspect of his religious outlook. The manner in which he cites the authority of the apostles is noteworthy; evidently by the time he wrote the apostles had arisen to high dignity. This trend has been mentioned. It has been observed in such works as "The Teaching of the Lord through the Twelve Apostles to the Nations," the Epistle of Barnabas, and the Pastorals. Indeed, it was not long after Jude was written that another pious leader put into writing the "Epistle of the Apostles." Finally, the use of Jude by the writer of 2 Peter puts the point beyond doubt: by the middle of the second century the word of the apostles was taken with great seriousness by Christian communities, and was used with great effect by Christian leaders.

What is seen in Jude is still more obvious in 2 Peter. The fact of pseudonymity, together with the studied attempt at verisimilitude, unmistakably points to a situation in which maturing Christianity is instructed by the figure of a leader long since dead, about whose memory weighty authority coheres. Appealing to Peter, the point is made explicit that his guidance will be valuable after his death: "I will hasten so that upon every occasion after my going away you may recall these things to memory" (1:15). This and the former epistle (the reference to 1 Peter is of course an attempt at verisimilitude) have been written "to stir up your sincere mind by putting you in remembrance" (3:1). Effort is made to invest the figure of Peter with reality; he is not only the author of this and the earlier epistle, but a brother of Paul (3:15), and one of those who heard God's voice when (as is said in coincidence with an item of gospel tradition) the writer was with Jesus "in the holy mountain" (1:18).

For this writer, Scripture (including Christian Scripture) is not merely authoritative, but is part of the institutional equipment of Christian groups. Another highly important point is that this Scripture is not open to private interpretation. It is the official interpretation of Scripture, such as the writer is supplying, which is authoritative. It is a reprehensible matter, in the writer's view, that some have misinterpreted Paul's letters, as they have wrongly handled the other Scriptures (3:16). Because of this, presumably, the rule is laid down — by the authority of Peter, of course — that no prophecy of Scripture is amenable to private interpretation (1:20). It is apparent that several categories are included here: the words of the prophets, the ordinances of the Lord which have come through the apostles (3:2), and the letters of Paul. Probably other apostolic writings, such as 1 Peter, are also in view.

Indeed, the library of Christian Scripture of which the writer of 2 Peter exhibits acquaintance is of astonishing range. He specifically mentions the letters of Paul, implying their use as a corpus, and alludes to 1 Peter. Since most of Jude is incorporated it is plain that this small work was known and appreciated. The allusion to the heavenly voice

(1:17) indicates the use of the Matthean gospel. The reference to Peter's predicted death strongly suggests the use of the Fourth Gospel in the form which possessed the epilogue of chapter 21, and this, in turn, suggests that the fourfold gospel was known. Certainly apocalyptic works were known (2:2, 11), and the particular references to the end of the age (3:7–13) and to the place of departed spirits (2:4f) demonstrate the writer's fondness for lore such as made up the writings which were for a time on the fringe of standard collections of Christian Scripture.

The situation which 2 Peter was written to meet seems to have been essentially the same as that faced by the writer of Jude. What difference appears in their ways of meeting it is due to this writer's greater intellectual capacity, even though this merely takes the form of authoritative use of Scripture for disciplinary purpose. Obviously he is clever and effective in deriving pragmatic meanings from Scripture, and it is an aspect of his leadership that he is able to lay these down as official interpretations with sufficient sanction to secure the control for which he labors.

These late works abandon creative experience in favor of patterned behavior based upon apostolic tradition and written Scripture. This conclusively indicates their witness to maturing Christianity. They use the authority of antiquity, of tradition, and of written word to secure sanction. Even a cursory reading shows the great gulf between the free abandon of spiritistic expression which characterized the early Pauline communities and the conventionalized living which is expected of church people by the writers of Jude and 2 Peter. Nor is there anything which corresponds to the richer and more broadly based experience which one finds in the life which lies back of the gospel pericopes. Adventurous living has given way to standardized behavior.

To be sure, the standard is high and strictly moral. It is further to be observed that 2 Peter has gone far in taking over Hellenized manners and culture. But it is plain that in securing stability and quasi-permanence for Christianity, much of the charm of the genuinely primitive Christianity was given up.

Second Peter thus exhibits a type of Christian living which bridged the development from the adventitious and the fortuitous expansion of early Christianity to the stable and permanently established movement which won its way in the ancient world by the absorption of competing groups. The issue with the sectaries was met by imposing of disciplinary control which, while not so strict as to repel large numbers, was yet sufficiently strong to bring into being the Catholic Christianity which appeared a generation later. The problems presented by the social and cultural relations with the people of the world in which the Christians lived were met by an increasing adaptation and adjustment. The presently emerging problems of explicit opposition were met as Christians increased in number. As yet, of course, these were not pressing problems.

Maturity may also be seen in the fact already emphasized, that Christians were able to introduce standards of measurement of orthodoxy and loyalty, and by the complementary fact that leaders were equipped with arguments for Christianity's defense. It should be remembered that 2 Clement appeared at about the time of 2 Peter; the former utilized the preacher's method, while the latter is the product of one whose abilities were in the realm of administration. Or, looking in the other direction, it was not long after the writing of 2 Peter that the formal literature of defense was in production. Second Peter appeared at the point of transition.

On the other hand, the more popular aspects of Christianity in the period of emerging maturity are to be seen in those works which the author of 2 Peter viewed with some distaste. While, as has been mentioned, he seems to have known and used some works which were on the fringe of standard use, it is a striking fact that the " apocryphal " gospel tradition, abundantly witnessed in 2 Clement (5, 11, 12), appears in 2 Peter only in its formulation of the *decensus* tradition (2:4 ff). Doubtless the luxuriant growth which is but faintly suggested by the known " apocryphal " gospels was distrusted, since it lent itself too readily to the private and unauthorized interpretation which the writer opposes.

It will be profitable to recall, also, that the period of Jude and 2 Peter was the period when the miscalled " Western " text reached its first flourishing.[5] The value of this observation appears when it is recalled that this " text " is truly apprehended as many popular texts, in which numerous items of tradition appear which brought into the gospel traditions so much of their legendary content. The most striking examples are the well-known stories of the woman taken in adultery and the man working on the sabbath. These remind one that popular texts (reflected in the authorities of the so-called Western text) were vehicles for the propagation of many items of gospel and apostolic tradition which were very like the elements of the apocryphal gospels and acts.[6]

It is in such perspective that the meaning of 2 Peter is perceived. It reflects the leadership which brought out of the diverse trends in middle second century Christianity the order which it achieved, the order which made for stability, organization and permanence. There is no value in regretting the loss of primitivity, any more than bemoaning the loss of the charm of infancy as the child becomes the youth and the youth becomes the adult. It is instructive to observe how Christianity grew; the processes by which its infancy and childhood were succeeded by sturdy maturity are not less important, even though they are usually thought to be less interesting, than its genetic relations and its beginnings.

It has been observed that early Christianity was characterized by a wide variety of types of religious living. This fact goes far to explain the trends which are observable in maturing Christianity. The life of the Palestinian communities could never have become the common pattern of Christians living in the widespread localities of the larger Mediterranean world. The people of the Palestinian communities were never numerous, and very quickly they became a small minority as the transition to gentile environments occurred. With no essential aspects of the religious life to distinguish them from their (Jewish) neighbors, it was inevitable that others than the Palestinian " Christians " would effect the distinctive qualities in the Christian movement. But equally inevitably the Pauline communities, unless they had changed rapidly and fundamentally, could never have established Christianity as a well-grounded religious movement. Their spiritism was individualistic; it would have been divisive in the earlier days, as Montanism was sectarian later in its reaffirmation of spiritistic experience. Only the adaptability of the Pauline communities permitted them to function use-

fully in the transition from a basically other-worldly movement to a social movement of this world.

As has been shown, the leadership which is exhibited in
the production and the organization of the gospel materials
is that in which the stabilizing forces of Christianity are to
be observed. Even of these there were elements which had
to be discarded. The enthusiasm for apocalyptic deliver-
ance had to be abandoned or replaced by another zeal. A
number of the social and moral standards of the leaders who
produced the gospels proved to be impractical, for example,
the radical antipathy toward wealth. But it is a fact of
central importance that there was in Christianity an adaptability which enabled it to effect needed changes. Now in
the period of the later books of the New Testament there
first appears that subtle and hardly definable quality which
came a little later [7] to characterize Catholic Christianity:
that quality of tolerance, of acceptance with broad sympathy,
of inclusiveness. The absorption of all sorts of people involved the attitude of tolerance of popular tendencies, so
that the fondness for popular miraculous tales and the attachment of marvelous stories to prominent persons received
adequate expression. Thus the apostles achieved their places
of distinction to the point that they were hardly below Jesus
as symbols about which the aura of authority developed.

The point at which positions of leadership came to possess
desirability is the turning point at which the growing stability of the Christian movement passed to that degree of
maturity which is seen at the mid-point of the second century. The increase in the number of Christians, together
with the latitude which was an inevitable concomitant of
inclusiveness, had the natural result that as an average was

lowered by numbers, so also the quality of leadership was less exceptional. Obviously the writer of the Pastorals was a lesser man than Paul, the writer of the Johannine letters than the writer of the Fourth Gospel, of Jude than the writer of Hebrews. Not that these were of low order, either in quality or ability. It is merely that there were essential differences in the Christian movement as a whole, and that these differences had far-reaching effects in particulars, including the outlook and the achievements of leaders. When, not long after, situations occurred which required heroic leaders, the Christian movement and the situations produced them. But the necessities of the middle second century did not produce a Tertullian, a Clement of Alexandria, a Hippolytus. They did produce Polycarp and Justin. These men were equal to their occasions.

It must not be forgotten that the appealing qualities of popular Christianity were at this very time expressing themselves in the production of still more stories of Jesus and of the apostles. These are the days when the Gospel according to the Hebrews was highly influential, when the figure of John was attracting a variety of adventurous experiences (in debate with heretics, surviving attempts to put him to death,[8] et cetera), and when the romantic and fanciful " acta " stories were springing up to invest the figure of every apostle with remarkable stature. Soon, as the almost contemporaneous Martyrdom of Polycarp shows, the cult of the martyrs was a recognized institution,[9] adding a wealth of detail to the rapidly growing reputation of the saints. Documents containing these traditions and stories presently had wide circulation. These stories and documents were so popular that they could not fail to attain widespread currency. Occasionally, as in Jude, 2 Peter and 2 Clement, one may catch a glimpse of them reflected in writings which have been preserved; it is a fair inference that these glimpses represent a mere fraction of their total currency.

These were the forces which led Christian officials and writers in the middle of the second century to make use of the legendary figures of the apostles to promote Christianity as they thought it should be developed. Doubtless it was easier for the people of the churches to revere a Paul, a Peter, or a Barnabas, men such as they had seen, than to depend solely upon a deified Lord for the concrete authority needed for the practical matters of the common life. There can be no doubt that the function of the host of intermediary saints, which attained such high development later, was effective in the days when the Christian movement was exhibiting the first signs of its emerging maturity.

It was thus easy and effective, as well as eminently useful, to articulate religious teaching in the variety of ways which are to be observed in these sources. Teaching was articulated in letters ascribed to Paul, Barnabas and Peter. Apocalyptic was even then shading over to the substitute which presently took its place, the martyrology.[10] Some of the basic conceptions of earlier apocalyptic had already given place to quite opposite Hellenistic conceptions: 2 Peter uses the term and the thoroughly Greek conception of Tartarus, and cites the first use of the chiliastic notion (2:4, 3:8), and the so-called *Apocalypse of Peter* has already gone the full length of transforming the conception of punishment after death from Jewish to thoroughly Greek terms.[11] New and popular stories of Jesus were appearing (in apocryphal gospels and in the various forms of the so-called Western text). Such new gospels as appeared differed from the now firmly established fourfold gospel in the direction of popular interests. The same popular interests expressed themselves particularly with reference to the apostles; it was now essential to show that the individual works of the fourfold gospel could be attached to or at least connected with apostles. It was not long after these days that the then orally current stories were written in the " acts " of the several apostles. Soon the high claim was made for a noble bishop that besides being a martyr he was a prophetic and an apostolic teacher (Mart. Pol. 16:2). It was already sufficient for an anonymous document of unusual form to have the title: " The Teaching of the Lord through the Twelve Apostles." Not yet, to be sure, was the homily of James ascribed to James of Jerusalem, nor was the Jude of the Epistle identified as the brother of that James. But in the pseudonymous letters of Paul, Barnabas and Peter the trend is sufficiently indicated.

The initial creative period in the growth of Christianity had indeed passed. Christianity, now spoken of by its leaders as such, had achieved solidarity. Consciousness of itself had led by this time to full consciousness of difference from others. The battle with Jewish opponents was long since over. At present there was in the absence of pressure from the State a period in which the major problems of maturing Christianity were internal. To be sure, already more than one sharp conflict with the officials of Roman conservatism had drawn lines between people of the churches and people of cults approved (or at least not disapproved) by the State. Functioning as a salvation cult, it was still advantageous for a Christian society to be able to point to similarities with others of such cults. The old apocalypticism had made the necessary concessions to Hellenistic culture and had receded into the background. There had been a general, if at first unconscious, acceptance of this world. No longer merely nor even primarily urban, cults of Jesus were now well distributed on all shores of the Mediterranean, usually well established to some distance inland.[12]

The measure by which to scale these phenomena is furnished when it is recognized that some of the Apologies were already in circulation, and that the best and most typical examples of this form were soon to appear. It is indicative of Christianity's past that the initial impulses in these works was the argument over the relative values of Christianity and Judaism (although it should be recognized that these arguments were made on the basis of literary, rather than experiential, awareness of Judaism; it should also be borne in mind that the arguments in favor of Christianity and in disparagement of Judaism were written by the same person — for the apologist Judaism was merely a man of straw set up only to be knocked down). Especially significant is the way in which the earlier of these, but of course most particularly such works as Justin's *Dialogue with Trypho* and his *Apology* with its supplement, reflect the advanced adaptation to contemporary Graeco-Roman culture. They plainly show that the Christian movement could now make a strong bid for recognition, both as a cult among other cults, and as a movement which was worthy of legal permission by the State. It was not long until the bid for recognition as a movement with cultural status was made in an abundant literature of (cultural) defense.

In their administration the churches were now directed by officials whose duties were specifically and definitely determined. Their offices brought social recognition of some sort. They also brought lucrative reward. For both these reasons offices were sought.

Leaders now looked back to find in tradition and in writings which had been produced by their own movement the necessary guidance in meeting new problems. The writings were used in collections; there were New Testaments beside the Old Testament.[18] Jewish Scripture had, indeed, been appropriated so completely that a Christian apologist could accuse Jews of mutilating, in their own interests, the writings which were regarded by Christians as really their own (Justin, *Dialogue*, lxxi-lxxiii; compare Pseudo-Justin, *Hortatory Address*, xiii).

Communication between far distant groups was maintained. This was affecting ecclesiastical administration; certain bishops were recognized as of right exercising large government. These not infrequently discussed questions of custom, of discipline, of teaching with one another,[14] so that more general conformity was appearing. It is significant that the status recognized as that of Catholic Christianity was reached in less than fifty years from the point here characterized (i.e., that marked by the appearance of the latest books of the New Testament) as that of maturing Christianity. Such a Christianity was able, when need arose, to grapple with the State. As early as the days of its emerging maturity Christianity's future was assured.

To close the study at this point necessarily requires the omission of a number of interesting factors. The rise of a Christian intellectualism worthy of the name was yet to occur; as yet no Origen, nor any Clement of Alexandria, had appeared. Second, the triumph over the State, although potentially prepared for, was yet to come. Third, the cleavage between East and West was not perceptible except as the variety which characterized nascent Christianity from its beginnings is plainly to be seen. However, Christianity as it matured was yet a Greek movement; Latin Christianity, if there was any such, was registered only in the private life and speech of those who were not in position to articulate the judgments and standards which are made by leaders.

However, the religious life which is seen in early Christian literature is the force which effected Christianity's integration in the Mediterranean world. To observe its expression in the variety of forms which are seen in Christianity's writings is to observe an organic growth. From it the student learns of the development from nascent Christianity to Christianity's maturity.

NOTES

PART ONE

BEFORE THE GOSPELS

I. BEGINNINGS

1. The reference is to the spiritistic behavior which certainly characterized members of the Pauline communities, probably characterized members of other Hellenistic communities, and was said to have characterized the primitive Palestinian disciples. See Case, *The Evolution of Early Christianity* (Chicago, 1914), 128ff.

2. The qualification is important; it is not to be concluded that aspects of behavior which are to be observed in cases of the noteworthy few characterized the many. It is of further importance to permit this distinction to occasion a broader generalization: there were varying types of experience and behavior; no one pattern was normative for all, nor was any pattern generally observed.

3. A scientific attempt to determine probability points in this direction, rather than in the direction suggested by Luke-Acts, in which there is a definite "theory" of Christianity's expansion. It is suggested by Luke-Acts that gentile Christianity was implicit in the teachings of Jesus, but that by divine direction the disciples were at first limited to Jerusalem and to Jews, so that the transition to gentile environments occurred only gradually. The very details of Luke-Acts itself contradict this, however. See Riddle, *Jesus and the Pharisees* (Chicago, 1928), 50–66.

4. Obviously the point of view maintained above uses the early chapters of the Acts section of Luke-Acts very critically. As was remarked in Note 3, these chapters develop a "theory" which is too logical and too schematic to be plausible. The view presented here is an attempt to infer from the sources a sequence which seems to be probable. It is more than doubtful that nascent Christianity was restricted to Jerusalem and to Jews, and was offered to native Hellenists only after it had reached Antioch.

II. THE PRIMITIVE PREACHING

1. See Dibelius, *Formgeschichte des Evangeliums* (Tübingen, 1933), 8–33; English translation by Woolf, *From Tradition to Gospel* (London, 1934), 9–36.

2. The meaning of the term "ecclesia" should not be regarded as indicating a uniform or a definitely organized group for every cult of disciples. However,

it is highly probable that groups were formed, whatever was their name or nature. There are later references to "synagogai" (James 2:2, Ignatius, Epistle to Polycarp 4:2, Hermas, Mandate XI, 9, 13, 14). But Paul's references to "the churches in Judea" (1 Thess. 2:14, Gal. 1:22) show that the association of believers into groups was not an exclusive feature of the Pauline communities.

3. It must be emphasized that these illustrations are not to be regarded as of universal reference. It must constantly be remembered that Pauline "Christianity" was not typical of all "Christianity."

4. The people of the "churches in Judea," doubtless nearly all of them Jewish, were very probably exceptions to this. However, they were in the minority in emerging Christianity from an early time.

III. PAUL

1. The point is made explicit in the "Western" text of Acts 18:25, which says that Apollos "had been instructed in the Lord's word in his own country."

2. This is stated by Luke-Acts, and, what is more significant, is a certain inference from Paul's letters.

3. See, for example, Charles, *Religious Development Between the Old and the New Testaments* (New York, undated), and Charles, *Eschatology: Hebrew, Jewish, and Christian* (London, 1913).

4. Herford, *Pharisaism; its Aim and Method* (London, 1912), *The Pharisees* (New York, 1924), *Judaism in the New Testament Period* (London, 1928); Abrahams, *Judaism* (London, 1910), *Studies in Pharisaism and the Gospels* (Cambridge, 1917, 1924); Dibelius, *Die urchristliche Überlieferung von Johannes dem Täufer* (Göttingen, 1911), *Die Geisterwelt im Glauben des Paulus* (Göttingen, 1909); Moore, *Judaism* (Cambridge, 1927–30).

5. See Enslin, "Paul and Gamaliel," *Journal of Religion*, 7(1927):360–375.

6. Case, "The Jewish Bias of Paul," *Journal of Biblical Literature*, 47(1928): 20–31.

7. Wendland, *Die hellenistisch-römische Kultur* (Tübingen, 1907), 19f.

8. Case, *The Evolution of Early Christianity* (Chicago, 1914), 110; K. L. Schmidt, *Die Stellung des Apostels Paulus im Urchristentum* (Giessen, 1924).

9. It is possible that the stories related in the latter volume of Luke-Acts are too schematic at this point also. Schwartz in a critical study of the "missionary journeys" concludes that the "first" and "second" are stories of one journey (E. Schwartz, "Zur Chronologie des Paulus," *Göttingische Nachrichten*, 1907, 263ff.).

IV. THE EARLIEST EXTANT CHRISTIAN WRITING

1. It is probable that too rigid an orthodoxy obtains in inferring the sequence of Paul's letters. The student's mind should be open to suggestion of new sequences. For example, my friend Dr. John Knox has fruitfully observed that the statistics of "fourteen years" in Galatians and 2 Corinthians indicate the

practical contemporaneousness of these two works ("Fourteen Years Later, A Note on the Pauline Chronology," *Journal of Religion*, 16(1936):341–49). The theory of an Ephesian or the Caesarean imprisonment being the situation of certain letters may indicate the need of revising traditional sequence.

2. The usual sequence of 1 and 2 Thessalonians and Galatians is followed. It does not appear that particular value results from the treatment of Galatians as the first Pauline letter; cf. Emmett, *St. Paul's Epistle to the Galatians* (London, 1912), Duncan, *The Epistle of Paul to the Galatians* (New York, 1934). On the other hand, it is an important element in a decisive point of view that Paul began to write only after he set foot on the continent of Europe.

3. The ancient argument concerning the destination of Galatians may be reviewed in Moffatt, *Introduction to the Literature of the New Testament* (New York, 1918), 90–101, a defense of the North Galatian theory, and in Burton, International Critical Commentary, *Galatians* (New York, 1920), xvii-xliv, a maintenance of the South Galatian theory.

4. References in the sources to Cephas and to Peter (the latter frequently with another name) suffice to raise a reasonable doubt that Cephas and Peter are the same person. See Lake, "Simon, Cephas, Peter," *Harvard Theological Review*, 14(1921):95–97. It is well, at all events, to use the particular name cited in the source.

5. Colwell, "Christianity a Gentile Religion in Galatians 2:14," *Anglican Theological Review*, 14(1932):42–47.

6. Since the Greek and corresponding Hebrew terms for "pronounce acquitted," "just," and "justness" are to a considerable degree forensic, it is essential to keep their quasi-technical sense in mind. See the extended Note on these terms in Burton, *op. cit.*, 460–474.

7. It is a point of essential distinction that to Paul the Torah was regarded almost exclusively in the statutory sense, which only in imperfect part indicates its true meaning. The fact largely accounts for Paul's antipathy to Torah. See Montefiore, *Judaism and St. Paul* (New York, 1915).

8. See Burton, *op. cit.*, 215, 510ff.; Lohmeyer, *Colossians* (Meyer Commentary) (Göttingen, 1930), 103ff.

9. The first appearance in the sources of a persistent problem: the relation of the spirit life and the moral life. See below, and Notes.

10. Riddle, "The So-Called Jewish Christians," *Anglican Theological Review*, 12(1930):15–33; Cadbury, "The Hellenists," in Lake and Cadbury, *The Beginnings of Christianity*, Vol. V (London, 1933), 59–74.

11. Ropes, *The Singular Problem of the Epistle to the Galatians* (Cambridge, 1929).

12. Ropes, *op. cit.*, and Lütgert, *Gesetz und Geist, eine Untersuchung zur Vorgeschichte des Galaterbriefes* (Gütersloh, 1909), *Freiheitspredigt und Schwärmgeister in Korinth* (ibid., 1908).

13. The logical contradiction of this is well pointed out by Enslin, *The Ethics of Paul* (New York, 1930), and by Andrews, *The Ethical Teaching of Paul* (Chapel Hill, 1934).

14. It is important to observe that in this discussion Paul is careful to distinguish between advice given on his own judgment and that which was "of the Lord" (1 Cor. 7:10, 11). Doubtless the distinction was based upon the difference in judgments obtained by the exercise of rational thought and those which came from spiritistic experience; Paul closes the discussion by insisting that he has "spirit of God" (7:40). It is probable, also, that the deprecation of marriage is to be taken much less as an indication of ascetic tendencies in Paul's life, but much more as an implication of his apocalyptic expectation.

15. It is a striking fact that the best attested reading implies the integrity of the twelve as a group during the "resurrection appearances." That is, this is a reflection of a genuinely primitive situation, antedating the reflection and theologizing which resulted in the articulation of the gospel traditions which characterize one of the twelve (why was it Judas?) as a traitor. The passage when so viewed is an instructive illustration of the methodological point that the gospel traditions are later and pragmatic (and in this case aetiological) stories.

16. The now generally accepted reconstruction of the Corinthian correspondence may be read in any competent handbook, e.g., Moffatt, *Introduction*, 108–130. The most influential dissent is registered by Windisch, *Der zweite Korintherbrief* (Meyer Commentary) (Göttingen, 1924).

17. See Enslin, *op. cit.*, 1–59.

18. This is a highly important contribution made by Andrews in the work cited and in "The Problem of Motive in the Ethics of Paul," *Journal of Religion*, 13(1933):200–215.

19. The questions of the integrity and of the destination of Romans should be carefully investigated and taken into account. They are fully discussed in Lake, *The Earlier Epistles of St. Paul* (London, 1911), 325–370.

20. See Case, *Journal of Biblical Literature*, 47(1928):29f., Ropes, "The Epistle to the Romans and Jewish Christianity" in Case (editor), *Studies in Early Christianity* (New York, 1928), 353, 365, and Andrews, *The Ethical Teaching of Paul* (Chapel Hill, 1934), 151.

21. This is discussed fully by Deissmann in a monograph, *Die neutestamentliche Formel 'in Christo Jesu'* (Marburg, 1892), and in his *Paulus* (English translation, *Paul*) (New York, 1926), *passim*.

22. The mystical background of the Pauline type of experience is excellently described in Willoughby, *Pagan Regeneration* (Chicago, 1927).

23. There is a large bibliography on this matter; it is reported to the date 1925 in Deissmann, *Paul* (London, 1926), 17, Note. An excellent discussion in English is in Duncan, *St. Paul's Ephesian Ministry* (London, 1929).

24. Lohmeyer, *Philippians*, and *Colossians-Philemon*, in the Meyer Commentary.

25. See, for example, beside standard handbooks of introduction and recent commentaries, the remarks in Lake, *Landmarks in the History of Early Christianity* (New York, 1922), 92ff., and Goodspeed, "The Place of Ephesians in the First Pauline Collection," *Anglican Theological Review*, 12(1930):189–212.

26. This may be considered as established in view of the discussion in Lohmeyer's *Colossians*.

27. Holtzmann, *Kritik der Epheser- und Kolosserbriefe* (Leipzig, 1927).

28. Goodspeed, *New Solutions of New Testament Problems* (Chicago, 1928), *The Meaning of Ephesians* (Chicago, 1933), and the article referred to in Note 25.

29. Lightfoot, *The Epistles of St. Paul: Philippians* (London, 1885), 40ff.

30. Lohmeyer, *Philippians*.

31. Lohmeyer, *Colossians*.

32. See the excellent statement in Willoughby, *Pagan Regeneration* (Chicago, 1927).

33. Weidinger, *Die Haustafeln* (Leipzig, 1928).

34. The distinction is emphasized by Lake, both by implication of the title of his earlier work, *The Earlier Epistles of St. Paul*, and expressly in his *Landmarks in the History of Early Christianity*, p. 93. There seems to be little point in the distinction, however. It is highly probable that the longer period of time between Paul's "conversion" and the writing of his first letter was the period for the development of his religious conceptions and convictions, rather than the briefer time which elapsed between the writing of his earliest and his latest letters. The data noted by Lightfoot, which make an earlier date for Philippians defensible, cannot easily be disposed of. The theories of an Ephesian imprisonment readily lend themselves to a reconsideration of the dates of the supposedly "later" letters.

35. E.g., in Charles, *Eschatology: Hebrew, Jewish, and Christian* (London, 1913), 461ff.

36. Not only the statements in Goodspeed, *The Meaning of Ephesians* (Chicago, 1933), but the excellent discussion of Philemon by Knox in *Philemon Among the Letters of Paul; A New View of Its Place and Importance* (Chicago, 1935) should be carefully noted.

37. There is a classical defense of this view by Ramsay in *Pauline and Other Studies* (New York, undated), 49–100.

V. NON–PAULINE CHRISTIANITY BEFORE THE GOSPELS

THE GOSPEL MATERIALS

1. This generalization is now a century old. First adumbrated by Lachmann in 1835, the demonstration was made by Weisse, *Die evangelische Geschichte kritisch und philosophisch bearbeitet*, 2 vols. (Leipzig, 1838) and by Wilke, *Der Urevangelist* (Dresden u. Leipzig, 1838).

2. A representative statement of a once very popular theory is that of Wright, *The Composition of the Four Gospels* (London, 1890), *A Synopsis of the Gospels in Greek* (London, 1896).

3. It is important to observe that "some" total is all that can be said; the "reconstructions" of "Q" varied widely in the detail of exactly how much or

what non-Marcan material should be considered as part of the "second source." This fatal variation is plainly shown in the representative Tables exhibited in Moffatt's *Introduction*, pp. 197–202, which should be carefully studied.

4. Burton, "Some Principles of Literary Criticism as Applied to the Synoptic Gospels," *The Decennial Publications* (Chicago, 1904).

5. Streeter, *The Four Gospels* (London, 1924); Taylor, *Behind the Third Gospel* (London, 1926).

6. A convenient "reconstruction" of this hypothetical document may be seen in *Theology*, 14(1927):133–164.

7. E.g., Bussmann, *Synoptische Studien*, 3 vols. (Halle, 1925–31).

8. Schmidt, *Die Stellung der Evangelien in der allgemeinen Literaturgeschichte* (Göttingen, 1923); reprinted from *Eucharisterion* (Göttingen, 1923).

9. Schmidt, *Der Rahmen der Geschichte Jesu* (Berlin, 1919).

10. Dibelius, *Formgeschichte des Evangeliums* (Tübingen, 1919, 33); Bultmann, *Die Geschichte der synoptischen Tradition* (Göttingen, 1921, 32).

11. Grant, *Form Criticism* (Chicago, 1934); see also the same author's *The Growth of the Gospels* (New York, 1933).

12. Albertz, *Die synoptische Streitgespräche* (Berlin, 1921).

13. The chapter on "The Primitive Preaching" should be carefully studied (German edition, pp. 8–34, English translation, pp. 9–36).

THE GOSPEL SOURCES

14. Bertram, *Die Leidensgeschichte Jesu und der Christuskult* (Göttingen, 1922).

15. Albertz, *op. cit.*

16. Riddle, "The Structural Units of the Gospel Tradition," *Journal of Biblical Literature*, 55(1936):45–58.

17. This has been recognized and generally admitted. See, for example, Moffatt, *Introduction*, 207–209, and Colani, *Jésus-Christ et les croyances messianiques de son temps* (Strasbourg, 1864).

18. As was remarked above, this is plainly shown by the Tables exhibited in Moffatt's *Introduction*, pp. 197–202.

19. Earlier works on this theory are mentioned in a study which applies it: Burney, *The Aramaic Original of the Fourth Gospel* (Oxford, 1922), 2f. The current application of the theory is made by Torrey, in *The Four Gospels* (New York, 1933).

20. See, for example, the criticism of a recognized Semitist, G. A. Barton, in the *Journal of Theological Studies*, 36(1935):357–373.

21. Riddle, "The Logic of the Theory of Translation Greek," *Journal of Biblical Literature*, 51(1932):13–30. A rejoinder was made by Burrows, *Journal of Biblical Literature*, 53(1934):13–30. See, further, Riddle, "The Aramaic Gospels and the Synoptic Problem," *Journal of Biblical Literature* 54(1935):127–138.

22. Bultmann, *op. cit.*, 393f.

23. The implied qualification is made for two reasons. First, it is significant

that some form of the "ur-Marcus" theory persistently recurs (cf. Goguel, "Luke and Mark, with a discussion of Streeter's theory," *Harvard Theological Review*, 26(1933):1–55). Second, the differences in the degree of similarity or closeness of parallel between Mark and another gospel insistently raise the question whether the relation which appears is between the given gospel and Mark, or between the given gospel *and some other current form of the independent pericope* (i.e., some form of the pericope which obtained independently of the Marcan gospel). This important question requires much further and very thorough research.

24. This point is familiar. It is made by such dissimilar approaches as those of Moffatt, *Introduction*, 207–209, and Bultmann, *op. cit.*, 393f.

25. All the sources of the Burton-Goodspeed theory may be seen in "reconstruction" in Sharman, *Records of the Life of Jesus* (Chicago, 1917), or may be identified by using a Burton-Goodspeed Harmony: *A Harmony of the Synoptic Gospels* (New York, 1917), *A Harmony of the Synoptic Gospels in Greek* (Chicago, 1920). A study of the Jerusalem Document has been published: Perry, *The Sources of Luke's Passion Narrative* (Chicago, 1919). The Matthean Document has been studied in an unpublished doctoral dissertation: *The Source of the Matthean Logia*, by R. R. Brewer, Ph.D. (University of Chicago Libraries, 1929).

26. The use of the plural in the Greek shows the intended purpose.

27. Riddle, *The Martyrs, A Study in Social Control* (Chicago, 1931), 20, 40, 45, 47f.

PART TWO

THE GOSPEL–MAKING PERIOD

VI. THE GOSPELS

1. This important point should be determined, if possible. It is discussed, either directly or by implication, in Riddle, "The So-Called Jewish-Christians," *Anglican Theological Review*, 12(1930):15–33, and in Cadbury, "The Hellenists," Lake and Cadbury, *The Beginnings of Christianity*, Vol. V (London, 1933): 59–74; cf. Schmidt, *Die Stellung des Apostels Paulus im Urchristentum* (Giessen, 1924), and Bauer, *Antiochea in der ältesten Kirchengeschichte* (Tübingen, 1909).

2. See especially the two last-named studies in the note above, and Case, *The Evolution of Early Christianity* (Chicago, 1914).

3. This is another point of basic importance. It is discussed fully and convincingly by Goodspeed in "The Origin of Acts," *Journal of Biblical Literature*, 39(1920):83–101 and in *New Solutions of New Testament Problems* (Chicago, 1927), 65–94. It is alluded to in Riddle, "The Logic of the Theory of Translation Greek," *Journal of Biblical Literature*, 51(1932):13–30. In a rejoinder

("Principles for Testing the Translation Hypothesis in the Gospels," *ibid.*, 53 (1934):13–30). Burrows writes as follows: "The Apocrypha and Pseudepigrapha likewise include works which are regarded by their modern editors as having been composed originally in Hebrew or Aramaic during the period with which we are concerned. According to the editors in Charles' edition the documents 'A' and 'B' in 1 Baruch, the books of the Martyrdom of Isaiah, the Assumption of Moses, and 2 Baruch, and the sources of 4 Ezra were all written in Hebrew during the first century." It must insistently be demanded how the judgment that certain Jewish books were written in Hebrew (if true) has anything to do with the question of the use of Aramaic. The question under discussion was whether there was *writing* in *Aramaic*.

4. See Riddle, "The Aramaic Gospels and the Synoptic Problem," *Journal of Biblical Literature*, 54(1935):127–138. It must be reiterated that the exponents of form- and social-history, many of them competent Semitists, fully take into account the Semitic element in the Greek of the gospels. But they are able to account for it by the fact that the pericopes of the gospel story had their first currency *while the gospel message was spoken*. The true significance of the statistics cited by Wellhausen, erroneously used by the exponents of the translation hypothesis, properly relates to this phenomenon. Wellhausen was one of the precursors of *Formgeschichte*.

5. This is a phase of the growth of collections of Christian Scripture. See, for example, Goodspeed, *The Formation of the New Testament* (Chicago, 1926), 33–41.

6. The full statement is worthy of quotation: "I did not, like the multitude, take pleasure in those who spoke much, but in those who spoke the truth, nor in those who related commandments belonging to others, but in those who rehearsed the commandments given by the Lord to faith, and proceeding to truth itself. If, then, anyone who had attended the elders came, I asked minutely after their sayings — what Andrew or Peter said, or what was said by Philip, or by Thomas, or by James, or by John, or by Matthew, or by any other of the Lord's disciples; which things Aristion and the Elder John, the disciples of the Lord, say. For I imagined that what was to be got from books was not so profitable to me as what came from the living and abiding voice" (Papias, Fragment I). Note that five sources of tradition are named before one of the traditional gospel writers is named, and that the testimony of such contemporaries as Aristion and the Elder John is rated as equal to the testimony of these.

7. For example, the martyr motif; cf. Riddle, "The Martyr Motif in the Gospel of Mark," *Journal of Religion*, 4(1924):379–410.

8. This is discussed in an important article, Burch, "Tragic Action in the Second Gospel," *Journal of Religion*, 11(1931):346–358.

9. The term is used in conscious dissent from the views of the exponents of *Formgeschichte*. These scholars are led by the strict logic of their method to insist that a gospel writer was merely a compiler, not an author. It is said, for example, that "Luke" was an author in "Acts," but merely a compiler in the Lucan gospel. The fact that the literary processes were essentially the same in

both sections of Luke-Acts denies this point. Much more important, however, is the fact that the effect secured by a gospel *as a whole* merits the gospel writer the title of author.

10. Professor Cadbury deserves much credit for the consistency of his treatment of Luke-Acts as a whole. See his *Style and Literary Method of Luke* (Cambridge, 1920) and *The Making of Luke-Acts* (New York, 1927). See also Riddle, "The Occasion of Luke-Acts," *Journal of Religion*, 10(1930):545–562.

11. The student should consult Dibelius, "Stilkritisches zur Apostelgeschichte," in *Eucharisterion* (Göttingen, 1923).

12. Compare also the discussion of sources in Harnack, *The Acts of the Apostles* (New York, 1909), 162–202.

VII. THE NON-GOSPEL LITERATURE OF THE GOSPEL-MAKING PERIOD

1. Goodspeed, *New Solutions of New Testament Problems*, "The Place of Ephesians in the First Pauline Collection," *The Meaning of Ephesians*.

2. Burkitt, *The Gospel History and Its Transmission* (Edinburgh, 1925), 289–323, and Knox, *Philemon Among the Letters of Paul* (Chicago, 1935), 38ff.

3. Knox, *op. cit.*, 40ff.

4. Lake, *The Earlier Epistles of St. Paul* (London, 1911), 325–370.

5. That Romans 16 was a letter of introduction of the deaconess Phoebe from the church of Cenchreae to the church at Ephesus is a familiar theory. See Deissmann, *Paul* (London, 1926). The theory has textual confirmation in the place of the doxology of Romans 16:25–27 in the Chester Beatty Papyri; see Sanders, *A Third-Century Papyrus of the Epistles of Paul* (Ann Arbor, 1935), 86.

6. "Josephus' Anticipation of a Domitianic Persecution," Case, *Journal of Biblical Literature*, 44(1925):10–20.

7. Goodspeed, "First Clement Called Forth by Hebrews," *Journal of Biblical Literature*, 30(1911):157–160, *New Solutions of New Testament Problems* (Chicago, 1927), 110–115; Riddle, "Hebrews, 1 Clement, and the Persecution of Domitian," *Journal of Biblical Literature*, 43(1924):329–348.

8. However, a recent defense of the idea is to be found in Wood (ed.), *Amicitiae Corolla* (London, 1933), 253–264.

9. Riddle, the work cited in Note 7 above and in "The Occasion of Luke-Acts," *Journal of Religion* 10(1930):545–562.

10. Torrey, "The Authorship and Character of the So-Called 'Epistle to the Hebrews,'" *Journal of Biblical Literature*, 30(1911):137–156, especially pp. 145ff.

11. Reagan, *The Preaching of Peter: the Beginnings of Christian Apologetic* (Chicago, 1923).

12. Riddle, *The Martyrs, A Study in Social Control* (Chicago, 1921), 104ff.

13. Riddle, "From Apocalypse to Martyrology," *Anglican Theological Review*, 9(1927):260–280, especially pp. 270ff.

14. Lohmeyer, *Die Offenbarung Johannis* (*Handbuch zum Neuen Testament*) (Tübingen, 1926); Riddle, *The Martyrs*, 164–170.

15. Charles, *The International Critical Commentary, Revelation* (New York, 1920), 1:364–367.

16. *Ibid.*, 1:lxviii–lxxxvi.

17. Riddle, "From Apocalypse to Martyrology."

18. Riddle, "The Occasion of Luke-Acts."

PART THREE

AFTER THE GOSPELS

VIII. A PICTURE OF POPULAR CHRISTIANITY

1. Riddle, "The Later Books of the New Testament: A Point of View and a Prospect," *Journal of Religion*, 13(1933):50–71.

2. Wilson, "The Career of the Prophet Hermas," *Harvard Theological Review*, 20(1927):21–62.

3. Wilson summarizes the major attempts; *op. cit.*, p. 21, Note.

4. It is regrettable that no translation of Hermas adequately exhibits its popular, unliterary style. The best translation, from this point of view, is that of Dibelius, in his edition of Hermas in the Lietzmann *Handbuch zum Neuen Testament, Die apostolischen Väter* (Tübingen, 1923).

5. Enslin, "A Second Century Pastor," *Crozer Quarterly*, 6(1929):278–298, especially p. 296.

6. Lake, *Landmarks in the History of Early Christianity*, 84ff.

7. Riddle, "The Messages of the Shepherd of Hermas," *Journal of Religion*, 7(1927):561–577.

8. Riddle, "The Structural Units of the Gospel Tradition," *Journal of Biblical Literature*, 55(1936):45–58.

9. See Lake, *The Stewardship of Faith* (New York, 1915), 125, 168–188.

IX. "BE READY TO SUFFER AS A CHRISTIAN"

1. Moffatt, *Introduction*, 318–344, especially pp. 323–327.

2. Canfield, *The Early Persecutions of the Christians* (New York, 1913).

3. Case, "Peter, Epistles of," Hastings' *Dictionary of the Apostolic Church* (New York, 1919), 2:201–209.

4. Riddle, *The Martyrs*, 156–163.

5. Gebhardt, *Acta Martyrium Selecta*.

6. Perdelwitz, *Die Mysterienreligionen und das Problem des 1 Petrusbriefes* (*Religionsgeschichtliche Versuche und Vorarbeiten*) (Giessen, 1911).

7. Streeter, *The Primitive Church* (New York, 1929), 121–141.

X. THE TEACHER EXPOUNDS HIS CODE

1. The *Didache* (and all other writings of the Apostolic Fathers cited in this study) may be conveniently read (in Greek and English) in Lake, *The Apostolic Fathers* (Loeb Library). The most thorough discussion of its literary problems is in Muilenburg, *The Literary Relations of the Epistle of Barnabas and The Teaching of the Twelve Apostles* (Marburg, 1929).

2. Riddle, "The Non-Septuagint Element in the Vocabulary of Paul," *Journal of Biblical Literature*, 47(1928):74–90.

3. See the excellent discussion by Ropes in *The International Critical Commentary, James* (New York, 1916), 10–16.

4. Goodspeed, *The Story of the New Testament* (Chicago, 1916), 100–105.

5. With reference to this general question, and particularly with reference to the specific matter of wealth and poverty, the discussion of Dibelius, *Der Brief des Jacobus* (Meyer Commentary) (Göttingen, 1921), is now classic.

6. This work is made conveniently accessible by Easton in his article, "Pseudo-Phocylides," *Anglican Theological Review*, 14(1932):222–228, from which the extracts cited are drawn.

7. See Weidinger, *Die Haustafeln* (Tübingen, 1928).

8. Attention is again called to the definitive discussion of this problem by Dibelius.

9. Moffatt, *Introduction*, 464.

XI. THE RISE OF SECTARIAN PROBLEMS

1. Goodspeed, *The Story of the New Testament*, 106–113.

2. The fullest study of the rise of the sects which takes modern findings into account is in an unpublished doctoral dissertation by R. E. Swenson, *The Rise of the Sects as an Aspect of Religious Experience* (University of Chicago Libraries, 1934).

3. I owe this suggestion to my friend, Dr. Alfred E. Haefner, of Waverly College, Waverly, Iowa.

4. Bultmann, "Stilanalyse des ersten Johannesbriefes," reprint from *Festgabe für Adolf Jülicher* (Tübingen, 1927), 138–158.

5. This suggestion, also, was made to me by Dr. Haefner.

6. If the full discussion of literary problems is desired, Lightfoot, *The Apostolic Fathers*, Vol. 1, Part 2 (London, 1885) is the classic source, pp. 222–414.

7. Riddle, *The Martyrs*, 60–75; Moffatt, "Ignatius of Antioch — A Study in Personal Religion," *Journal of Religion*, 10(1930):169–186.

8. This is said even though the opposite is maintained in the article by Lohmeyer, "Ueber Aufbau und Gliederung des ersten Johannesbriefes," *Zeitschrift für die Neutestamentliche Wissenschaft*, 27(1928):225–263.

9. Moffatt, *Introduction*, 589–593; Dibelius, "Johannesbriefe," *Die Religion in Geschichte und Gegenwart*, Vol. 3 (Tübingen, 1929), 346–350.

XII. EPISCOPAL CORRESPONDENCE

1. This feature of Ignatius' Epistle to Polycarp appears in section VI, which is obviously not appropriate as advice to a bishop, e.g., " Give heed to the bishop, so that God may also give heed to you." Indeed, the entire section presents its teaching in plurals. Sections IV and V are almost of the same color; they are hardly relevant as teaching directed to the bishop.

2. Harris, *Testimonies,* 2 vols. (Cambridge, 1916, 1920).

3. There have been recent studies of Ignatius, however: Richardson, *The Christianity of Ignatius of Antioch* (New York, 1935), Schilling, *The Mysticism of Ignatius of Antioch* (Philadelphia, 1933).

4. Lake, *The Apostolic Fathers,* Vol. 1.

XIII. THE GROWTH OF CHURCH RULES

1. If it were necessary to emphasize the lack of uniformity in church orders, the point would be sufficiently made clear by Streeter, *The Apostolic Church* (New York, 1929).

2. P. N. Harrison, *The Problem of the Pastoral Epistles* (London, 1921), is of the highest value as an exhibit of the statistical phenomena by which the questions of the integrity and the authorship of the Pastorals are to be determined. It is singularly weak, however, in that by limiting its objective to the proof that there are genuine Pauline fragments as sources in the Pastorals, it fails to account for what is obviously their major element, i.e., the pseudepigraphical " remainder."

3. Such is the view offered by Michaelis, *Die Gefangenschaft des Paulus in Ephesus und das Itinerar des Timotheus* (Gütersloh, 1925).

4. For full information see Harnack, *Marcion, das Evangelium vom fremden Gott* (Leipzig, 1921).

5. The later fulminations of Tertullian indicate the furore occasioned by Marcion's treatment of Scripture. To be sure, Tertullian's *Against Marcion* was written later, and it is manifestly wrong to regard it as an objective treatment from which Marcion's tenets may be objectively reconstructed. For example, modern research seriously discounts the accusation that Marcion made a thoroughgoing " expurgation " of his Gospel and Apostle sections of his Christian Scripture. And obviously Tertullian's statement that Marcion " rejected " the Pastorals begs the question; Tertullian gives no evidence to prove it.

6. See, for example, Epistle of Barnabas, 9:7-9.

7. Allegorical interpretation was developed by the Greeks. Not only does Philo illustrate the currency of allegorical interpretation in Alexandria, but Plutarch does the same thing, e.g., in his *Of Isis and Osiris.* This is excellently discussed by Rist, *Apuleius the Priest and Plutarch the Theologian* (unpublished dissertation, University of Chicago Libraries, 1934).

8. Harnack, " Marcion and the Marcionite Churches," *Encyclopedia Britan-*

nica, 11th ed., Vol. 17, 691–693; cf. *History of Dogma* (London, 1924), Vol. 1, 270, " It is very probable that 1 Timothy 6:20 — an addition to the Epistle — refers to Marcion's Antitheses." Harnack's judgment that the verse is an addition to the Epistle merely means that he was not willing to consider as late a date as this would indicate for the Epistle as a whole. There is no objective evidence that it is a later interpolation.

9. Muilenburg, *op. cit.*

XIV. MATURING CHRISTIANITY

1. Cf. Goodspeed, *New Solutions of New Testament Problems* (Chicago, 1927), 29–49.

2. Goodspeed, *Die aeltesten Apologeten* (Göttingen, 1915).

3. Conveniently illustrated in James, *The Apocryphal New Testament* (Oxford, 1924), 1–227.

4. Gebhardt, *Acta Martyrium Selecta* (Berlin, 1902).

5. This highly important matter is now receiving adequate attention in contemporary textual criticism. A significant contribution has been made by Clark in his *The Acts of the Apostles* (Oxford, 1933). See also Sanders, " The Egyptian Text of the Gospels and Acts," *Harvard Theological Review* 27(1933):77–98; Goodspeed, " The Letter of Jesus Christ and the Western Text," *Anglican Theological Review,* 15(1933):105–114 and Riddle, " Textual Criticism as a Historical Discipline," to appear in *The Anglican Theological Review,* 18 (1936).

6. " The Structural Units of the Gospel Tradition," *The Journal of Biblical Literature,* 55(1936):45–58.

7. It was not long after the time of the writing of the latest books of the New Testament that the Muratorian Fragment and the writings of Irenaeus, the earliest reflections of Catholic Christianity, appeared.

8. Traditions cited in Irenaeus, *Adv. Haer.,* 3:1:1, 3:3:4; Tertullian, *de praescr. Haer.,* 36; Clement of Alexandria, *Quis Div. Salv.* xlii, *Acts of John, passim;* Jerome, *Comm. on Matthew,* 20, 23; Augustine, *Tract. in Joh.,* cxxiv, 2.

9. *Op. cit.,* 17:3, 18:2, 3, 19:1, 2.

10. Riddle, " From Apocalypse to Martyrology," *Anglican Theological Review,* 9(1927):260–280; *The Martyrs, A Study in Social Control* (Chicago, 1931), 133ff.

11. This is established by Dieterich, *Nekyia usw.,* (Leipzig, 1893).

12. This generalization is indicated not only by the statement of Pliny's letter to Trajan (to the effect that Christianity has spread to the rural districts) but also by the early currency of Christianity in areas on the southern shores of the Mediterranean.

13. The plural is used advisedly; there were several New Testaments, from Marcion's to the highly inclusive New Testaments of Alexandria.

14. Polycarp's visit to Rome and his disagreements on certain points in discussion with Bishop Anicetus furnish an example.

INDEX

SUBJECTS AND PERSONS

Abraham, 30

Abrahams, Israel, 16

acta literature, 226, 228

" Acts," book of, 214

acts, apocryphal, 214

Acts of the Scillitan Martyrs, 147

Adam, 44

adaptability, Christianity's, 5

Aegean locale of Luke-Acts, 87

Aesklepius, 70, 71, 94

Africa, 51

agape, 149, 173

age, end of the, 178

Ahikar, 160

Alexandria, 12, 15, 23, 51, 119, 120, 202, 210, 213

Alexandrian literature, 124

allegorical interpretation, 212, 213

allegorical method, 30, 202, 210; use by Jewish scholars, 210

Andronicus, 11

anti-gentile polemic in Matthew, 102

anti-Gnostic polemic, 59

anti-Jewish polemic, 54, 59, 79, 80; in Matthew, 101, 102

anti-Judaism, 93, 211

Antipas, 129

antinomians in the Pauline communities, 32

Antioch, 29, 183; bishop of, 176

Antiochene locale of Matthew, 87, 93

Antitheses, Marcion's, 209

Apocalypse, the, 124, 138; of Ezra, 119

Apocalypse of Peter, 178, 228

apocalyptic, 6, 7, 16, 219, 225, 227,

228; disuse of, 128; form, modification of, 126; Jewish, 8, 9; literature, 221; messianism, 9, 17; section of *Didache,* 157

apocalypticism, 26

apocrypha, 211

apocryphal Acts, 214

apocryphal gospels, 73, 82, 83, 99, 214, 217, 223, 227

apocryphal gospel tradition, 223

Apollos, 11, 12, 13, 15, 32, 34

apologetic, Christian, 121; Christian, beginnings of, 120

apologetic narratives, 124

apologies, 217, 229

Apology, Justin's, 121

apostles, 11, 38, 41, 220; legendary figures of, 221; ordinances of, 185, 186

Apphia, 11, 60

Aquila, 11

Aramaic, 40, 76; sources of the gospels, 76

Archippus, 60

Aristarchus, 59

Aristion, 150, 151

Ascension of Isaiah, 119

asceticism, 33

Asia, 25, 213; Christianity in, 194

Asia Minor, 215

Asian churches, 171, 181, 183, 184

Asian locale of the Fourth Gospel, 87

Assumption of Moses, 219

Athens, 26

Attis, 94

SOURCES